# LION-HUNTING
IN
SOMALI-LAND

CLOSE QUARTERS. "HE WAS ABOUT TO SPRING WHEN I PULLED THE TRIGGER." (See p. 29.) [Frontispiece.

# LION-HUNTING

IN

# SOMALI-LAND

ALSO

*AN ACCOUNT OF "PIGSTICKING"
THE AFRICAN WART-HOG.*

BY

CAPTAIN C. J. MELLISS,

9TH BOMBAY INFANTRY.

WITH ILLUSTRATIONS BY CECIL ALDIN, AND FROM
PHOTOGRAPHS BY THE AUTHOR.

## Peter Capstick, Series Editor

ST. MARTIN'S PRESS
NEW YORK

*To the Reader:*

The editors and publishers of the Peter Capstick Adventure Library faced significant responsibilities in the faithful reprinting of Africa's great hunting books of long ago. Essentially, they saw the need for each text to reflect to the letter the original work, nothing have been added or expunged, if it was to give the reader an authentic view of another age and another world.

In deciding that historical veracity and honesty were the first considerations, they realized that it meant retaining many distasteful racial and ethnic terms to be found in these old classics. The firm of St. Martin's Press, Inc., therefore wishes to make it very clear that it disassociates itself and its employees from the abhorrent racial-ethnic attitudes of the past which may be found in these books.

History is the often unpleasant record of the way things actually were, not the way they should have been. Despite the fact that we have no sympathy with the prejudices of decades past, we feel it better—and indeed, our collective responsibility—not to change the unfortunate facts that were.

—Peter Hathaway Capstick

LION HUNTING IN SOMALILAND. Copyright © 1991 by Peter Hathaway Capstick. All rights reserved. Printed in the United States of America. No part of this book may be used or reproduced in any manner whatsoever without written permission except in the case of brief quotations embodied in critical articles or reviews. For information, address St. Martin's Press, 175 Fifth Avenue, New York, N.Y. 10010.

Library of Congress Cataloging-in-Publication Data

Meliss, C. J.
   Lion hunting in Somaliland / C.J. Meliss.
      p.   cm.
   ISBN 0-312-05463-7
   1. Lion hunting—Somalia.   2. Lion hunting—Ethiopia.   I. Title.
SK305.L5M45   1991
799.2′774428—dc20                                                    90-49170
                                                                                       CIP

First Edition: January 1991
10 9 8 7 6 5 4 3 2 1

## LIST OF ILLUSTRATIONS.

|  | TO FACE PAGE |
|---|---|
| CLOSE QUARTERS | *Frontispiece* |
| A WADI | 7 |
| MY FIRST LIONS | 32 |
| "I HAD SPENT SEVERAL DAYS IN THESE PLEASANT WILDS" | 38 |
| A LION ON THE PROWL | 55 |
| A HALF-HOUR'S BAG | 96 |
| AFTER A FAREWELL DAY WITH THE LIONS | 120 |
| "JUMPING QUICKLY ASIDE, I RAN THE SPEAR WELL HOME INTO HIS RIBS" | 131 |

# EDITOR'S NOTE TO THE REPRINT EDITION

Today's Somalia could have been nothing but confused in the number of names it had, and the quantity of masters before it achieved independence and the standard moniker "Somali Democratic Republic."

Originally just basking in the warm, coral-studded Indian Ocean and the still warmer Gulf of Aden, its some 67,000 square miles were the finest East Africa could offer to the British sporting tourist and hunter before Kenya came on line at the turn of the century.

Somalia, Somaliland, Somali-land, The Somali Republic; it was all the same place give a jot or tittle on the international map, and it was the real home of East African safaris. Long before Kenya, Uganda and Tanganyika became the bush equivalent of The Grand Tour, Somaliland was the plum for adventurous sport. It was sport now regarded as "not done," but the British brought it to us, the safari leave or holiday from, essentially, India, where British forces were headquartered at Simla. The sporting tradition of Somalia was basically that of the British officers, certainly typified

## EDITOR'S NOTE

by Captain C. J. Melliss of the 9th Bombay Infantry. There were many lions, which predated heavily upon herds of the Somali; and, of course, the ubiquitous warthog, which was looked on as the equivalent of the Indian boar, Sus scrofa, and equal candidate for pig-sticking.

There are eight major books in my library that deal with Somaliland. Perhaps there are others, but I would recommend these should you wish to pursue the subject. Of course, the material on Somaliland is, perforce, limited much more than that of Kenya and the other classic East African gamelands, but Somaliland has, at least, no literary flies on it. It was really the second area of safari activity beyond that of brother officers in South Africa and environs.

Possibly the first book of interest is that of Captain G.H.C. Swayne, Royal Engineers, written about his experiences in Somalia from 1885 to 1893. Entitled *Seventeen Trips through Somaliland*, and printed in 1895, it is perhaps the first to concur with the British victory at Omdurman, in the Sudan, which was a crashing win over the Mahdi, sort of a Khomeini of his day. The only criticism of the battle by the general and ordinance staff was the terrible amount of ammunition used to kill the wounded. Yet, the British are generally anti-bloodsport today. In 1894, leading a year by publication date the book you are now reading, Lord Wolverton's book, *Sport in Somaliland* came out

# EDITOR'S NOTE

also, although it is rather a slim tome. Count Potocki (pronounced Potoski) did his excellent work, *Sport in Somali-Land*, with the immortal Rowland Ward as publisher in a run of only 200, in 1900. Obviously, I am pleased to have a fine copy. From this date there was something of a gap until 1908 when, of all people, Agnes Herbert came out with *Two Dianas in Somaliland*--a fine book. Miss Herbert and her female pal slew lions and rhino under the toughest of conditions in Somalia, eventuating the death of some of their staff and a mauling for Miss Herbert. In 1913, A.H.E. Mosse, Captain in the Indian Army and a fellow of the Royal Zoological Society, did the last book of importance on Somalia, *My Somali Book*. Should you be as entranced by the country as Melliss' book presents the land and the people, I recommend the above.

Melliss was roughly typical of the British officer that came out into what was then British Somaliland. Of course, the Italians had collected a very small piece for themselves, but it was not nearly the size of the British holdings until Italy invaded it in 1936 and the British responded in 1941 with their own successful invasion, making a trust area of Somaliland.

As might be imagined, the British brought those sports they practiced in India with them, the lion taking the place of the tiger and the warthog that of the Indian boar. They called their

## EDITOR'S NOTE

professional hunters shikaris, as they were known in India, although they were more guides than hunters, spooring and finding their way through the terrain and generally acting as assistant to the hunter.

The English way of hunting was actually old by the time that Indian officers came to Somaliland. During the Second Boer War men of the status of Baden-Powell, founder of the Boy Scouts, even wrote a book on the subject of pig-sticking in Africa. There is probably no sport more represented by hog-hunting (as some purists would call it) than spearing pigs of nearly any description. It was no different with Melliss, who devotes the last chapters of his book to the sport.

I really couldn't say why the pastime, now defunct, appeals to me so. I would rather handle a charging lion any day than to board a recalcitrant horse that disliked me. Yet, the British thought, possibly with good reason, that pig-sticking was the ideal practice for war, especially for lancers, but one must bear in mind that most British infantry officers were mounted also.

Still, the Melliss book is mostly about lion hunting under rather hairy circumstances. We can intelligently surmise that Melliss had killed tigers in India (where man-eaters take about 3,500 people a year despite their "endangered" status) as well as having been an enthusiastic hog-hunter. Certainly his adventures on foot with wounded warthogs are enough to raise the hackles of the armchair reader

# EDITOR'S NOTE

quite sufficiently.

I have had considerable experience with warthogs myself, and woe betide the hunter who takes them lightly! They are every bit as dangerous as the European and Indian boars, and have much larger tushes or tusks, which whet upon each other so they are always as sharp as a pair of shears. I have been charged by warthog, and although considered relatively harmless in front of an express rifle, their ire can be monumental. Of course, sticking a spear into one of the family is guaranteed to make them a bit upset.

It really is a shame to me that the days of "a noble hog," <u>jhow</u> and <u>jheel</u> has gone, as have the tent camps of a big meet of officers vying for "first spear." But perhaps it really is not dead; it lives in the memories of such as Melliss in this grand book of hunting.

--PETER HATHAWAY CAPSTICK

# LION-HUNTING
IN
SOMALI-LAND

# LION-HUNTING IN SOMALI-LAND.

NOT long ago I made a shooting trip from India some two hundred miles or so into the interior of Somali-land. By P. and O. I reached Aden, and thence a wretched little trading-steamer took me by a circuitous route, *viâ* Perim, along the Somali coast. We put in at the ancient port of Zaila, where I landed, to see the place in which I had done five months' pleasant exile some half-dozen years before, "pigsticking" the wart-hog over the surrounding grass country. How unchanged it all was. The dreamy stillness, the ceaseless wash of the quiet sea, the cloudless blue above, the few houses of white coral rock, glaring white in the eternal sunshine, standing high above the dark reed huts of the Somalis, the Consulate facing the sea, with the English flag floating lazily over it, the Indian sepoy on sentry-go hard by. Nothing seemed changed. Yes, there was a change. Our flag alone waved there. I remembered the time when French and Egyptian were there too, and when the intrigues and blusterings of the former and the fights between English and French factions amongst the Somalis had enlivened the place immensely. But we had cleared them out since then, it appeared, and a sleepy peace seemed to reign over Zaila. Then, further down the coast, to the open roadstead of Bulhār. Here the coast line seems to stretch away as far as the eye can see in an unbroken line of yellow sand, fringed with the white foam of the breakers as they roll in from the gulf. Bulhār is purely a Somali trading settlement, consisting of a large collection of reed-mat huts pitched in the plain looking on to the broad, glittering, blue stretch of the open sea. Behind it a bush-covered country trends away in a yellow haze to a dim range of mountains. It is a wild spot, with a wild history of its own; for, thrice in the last few years it has been devastated by fire, cholera, and the spear of a hostile tribe — the bloodthirsty Eesa, who swooped down on it one night and slaughtered its inhabitants wholesale. On the third day I reached Berbera, heartily glad to escape from that fearful ship with its vile food, crowds of noisy natives, and its antediluvian monsters of black beetles. Two busy days at Berbera enabled me to get together a caravan, or "kāfila," as it is called in the country, of ten camels, twelve Somalis—seven of whom I armed with rifles—and two donkeys, whose ultimate purpose was to stand as bait for lion. Besides the provisions, which amounted to about 1,000 lbs. of rice, half that quantity of dates, and over 100 lbs. of ghee, a two months' supply for the party, there were numbers of other things to be thought of: saddle equipments for the camels, tobacco and clothes for presents, cooking-pots and shoes for the men, axes for making zarebas, water-casks and ropes, and many things besides, which, with the assistance of an Arab merchant of the place, named Mahomed Hindi, a very honest fellow, I got together. Finally, the purchase of an Abyssinian pony, at an exorbitant price, completed my preparations. One afternoon, out of a seeming chaos of multifarious packages strewing the ground, bad-tempered camels loudly complaining, and the cheery shouts of my noisy Somalis, a well-loaded kāfila was evolved in a wonderfully short time, and moved off a little before sunset for the first long march across the maritime plain.

I started the next morning at daybreak for a ride of some twenty-two miles across the stony, maritime plain, towards some distant low-lying hills, beyond which the kāfila would have halted. The country over which I rode was not inviting. Right up to the line of bare, yellow hills stretching along my left, to the sea which glittered a bright blue on my right, the plain was covered with nothing but wiry, stunted bush, and seemed devoid of life, except for an occasional gazelle, which would break away in bounds from beneath the shade of some bush, and then stand gazing at us at no great distance, offering a shot; or the squirrel-like field-rat, that whisked down their innumerable holes at our approach. It was a long, hot march, for my Somali guide was not mounted, and I soon preferred to walk myself than to sit baking in the saddle. The fierce sunshine ran in quivering lines of heat along the bare, stony plain, and it was a pleasant relief to look away to the cool, blue line of the sea I was leaving behind me. However, the weariest march has an end, and at last, early in the afternoon, I came upon my kāfila, halted in a dry, rocky "wadi," for so the river-beds in the country are called. Here I rested for a few hours, and then marched to another wadi six or eight miles further on, where we encamped for the night. My intention was to push on as fast as possible, as my time was limited, and I wished to hunt in the waterless plateau called the "Haud," which stretches through a great extent of Somali-land, its nearest edge from where I was being some hundred and fifty miles distant.

I marched next morning at dawn, halting a short while at noon to rest men and animals, and then moving on again until sunset. Thus I continued to push on, making double marches daily, while the country after a few days improved greatly. The maritime plain was left behind, and during the third day's march we found ourselves in a well-wooded country, amidst an amphitheatre of brown, rocky hills, on the sides and tops of which grew the dark-green, umbrella-shaped mimosa tree. Ahead of us towered the Lion Mountain (Gān-libah), the highest point of the thickly wooded Golis range, which lay along our left. The stony track we followed frequently led us across the sandy beds of the numerous wadis which intersect the country. In their stretches of white sand, between walls of rock or thick borders of tree and bush jungle, are the most charming bits of scenery. Creepers of all kinds in luxuriant growth fall in festoons from date-palm and mimosa tree; numbers of birds, some of brilliant plumage, fill the jungle along the banks with life; here and there dark-green patches of reeds stand up in the white, sandy bottoms, where pools of water, often with fresh, green grass growing about their margins, give the brightest of touches to these most picturesque wadis.

To stroll rifle in hand along the bed of a wadi in the quiet of the evening had a great fascination for me. A growing stillness seemed to creep over the jungle as the day waned, broken only by the sudden call of some bird from amongst the bushes, or the wailing cry of a jackal.

At such an hour what might one not chance

A WADI. [p. 7.

upon? Tracks of various antelope, wild boar, leopard, and hyæna crossed one's path. As one came softly round some bend in the wadi's winding course, revealing new vistas of its wild scenery, often the hyæna would hasten its skulking footsteps across the sand, or the wild boar dash alarmed from the pool. At such an hour the king of beasts himself might be met with, prowling forth to seek his food; for so I have more than once struck the tracks of his great paws clearly written along the sandy river-bed.

Our way led constantly upwards, though the ascent was hardly noticeable. Yet after a few days I found the climate cooler. The dark thunderclouds that rested on the Lion Mountain, and the brown, deliciously cool water that rushed down the gulleys near the track, told of the rainy season that was setting in—a point on which I was most anxious, for without the rains it would be impossible to hunt in the interior of the Haud. Skirting the Golis range, at a distance of some miles, my route continued with so constant an ascent that, on the fourth day, when I had covered about ninety miles, looking back to the massive head of Gān-libah, we seemed to be on a level with it. The general aspect of the country outside the wadis was rough and stony, with an open jungle of bush and flat-topped mimosa trees, above which the reddish brown earth columns of numerous anthills caught the eye.

We were now marching towards a low mountain wall, above which two rounded peaks rose outlined against the sky, reminding one of the approach to Rider Haggard's mysterious country in "Solomon's Mines." The very name of the peaks, "Naso Hablod," meaning in Somali the breasts of a girl, adds to the resemblance. Game now became more plentiful, small herds of gerenook (*gazella walleri*), awal (*gazella soemmerringii*), and dhero (*gazella naso*) were constantly seen, often grazing within rifle shot. Two long marches brought us to the peaks of Naso Hablod, where we crossed its mountain ridge next morning. I was now getting well into the country, and frequently news of lion from some passing Somali tempted me to turn aside from my route, but I held on. We usually marched at earliest dawn. Some time before the pale light grew in the Eastern sky, under a bright moon, the camp was broken up. I would be awakened out of a blissful sleep by the vilest row on earth, the grunting, groaning, bubbling complaints of camels being loaded up. Sleep fled before such nerve-jarring sounds, and I was out of my tent in no time, and whilst I became the better for a cup of cocoa and some chupattis, my tent was struck and packed with my other belongings, and the kāfila was ready to march at the first streak of dawn.

How pleasant it was walking through the jungle ahead of the string of camels, gun in hand, in the delicious cool of the dawn, for the animal world was up too. Constantly the dainty little sand-antelope (*neotragus sp.*) would spring away through the bushes at my approach. These charming little creatures, called in Somali-land " dĭk-dĭk," in size scarcely as big as an English hare, are the most dainty miniatures of the antelope race. They are ever in pairs of male and female, are much alike, except that the male has two tiny horns about an inch or two long, with a brown tuft of hair between them. Their skins vary in colour from a silvery grey to a russet brown. Flocks of guinea-fowl would scuttle off into the bush uttering their metallic cry; the bustard, too, would be up taking a stately constitutional, and more than once fell a victim for the pot. On the track, worn by the feet of generations of camels, some days we would meet with small parties of Somalis making their way to the coast, their strings of camels laden with skins of cows and goats, for which they found a market at Berbera. In front of the kafila marched one or two Somalis, one of whom invariably holds the nose-string of the leading camel in order to keep up the pace, which is about three miles an hour. Others sauntered along the line, several spears on the shoulder, a circular shield of hide on his arm, a white, or, rather, dirty white, bit of cotton sheeting wrapped, toga-like, about his body. His hair, sometimes short, black, and curly, sometimes in long, crinkly ringlets, bleached a light red, or, in the intermediate stage, plastered with a white mud, the Somal of the interior is a wild enough looking fellow. The women wear some sort of dark blue garment, usually displaying a great deal of their breasts. The married woman ties her hair up in a similar-coloured bit of cloth, while the "gubats" (maids) wear theirs in oily-looking plaits. They are much less picturesque than the men, and a good-looking one is a rarity. They usually bring up the rear of a kāfila, driving some fat-tailed sheep, goats, and a donkey or two before them. It was a source of wonder to me how the decrepit old women who were often with these kāfilas were able to make the long marches, which is a *sine quâ non* of travel in Somali-land. On one occasion I did pick up a miserably old woman lying exhausted and apathetic on the wayside, who had been abandoned by her considerate people to follow on the best way she could, since she could no longer keep up with her kāfila. Very tough, indeed, some of those marches were. Often we had to trudge for some distance along the hot, glaring bed of a wadi, sinking at every footstep in its soft sand. I was always very ready for the noonday halt to stretch myself out on a soft spot in the shade of bush or tree, and devour anything my indefatigable cook Ismail, a Somali, produced. As for the Somalis, they took little food until sundown. Some would sleep, others wash at the pools, or plaster their heads with a certain kind of earth found in the wadis, which bleached the hair a light red, a form of vanity much in mode amongst the young men.

Mightily glad, too, was I when, at sunset, sometimes when night was closing down on us, the long string of camels would be brought to a halt in the sandy bed of a wadi near the water-holes, or in the jungle beside the track if water were still distant. In a trice the camels are brought to their knees, and their loads strew the ground; the ungainly beasts get on to their long legs again, and stalk off, much relieved, into the gathering gloom to feed off the surrounding bushes, in charge of one of the men, whose white-clad figure, spear on shoulder, might be seen standing on some mound or anthill watching the grazing beasts. Some of the men are cutting down thorn-bushes to form a zareba round our encampment, others are pitching my tent, here they are lighting a fire, over which a big pot, full of rice and ghee, the men's dinner, will soon be boiling. The hearty way a Somali works is most refreshing. No matter how hot or long the day's march, or the thunderstorms at sunset that often drenched us before we could get up our encampment, soaking the camels' saddle-mats, which were their only bedding, yet there was always a laugh in them, and they would set to work with a will, usually singing in chorus to some chant set up by one of them. In a wonderfully short time we have settled down for the night. The camels have been driven in and made to lie down by the tying-up of a foreleg. Round the fire my men are sitting, a cheery group, eating their dates and rice. An hour later, as I look outside my tent before turning in, all has grown still. A bright moon shines on the forms of my men, stretched out asleep on the ground; on the circle of quaint, mis-shapen backs and long necks of the kneeling camels; on the solitary, white-clad figure of the sentry, as he stands, rifle in hand, near the dying fire, crooning to himself some Somali song, invariably of mournful note. The melancholy cry of the jackal, or the weird howl of the hyæna, is borne along on the night air, or, maybe, the grey shadows of their skulking forms pass in the moonlit jungle as they prowl outside our thorn-fence. Some such scene have I looked out upon many a night under the Southern Cross in the wild land of the Somal.

After passing Naso Hablod, we travelled along a ridge, the ground on either side sloping away from us into broad, thickly-wooded valleys, beyond which rose other ridges of high ground, their slopes dark with mimosa-tree jungle. My head shikari, Jama, told me that it was in one of the wadis close by where Mr. Ingram was killed by an elephant. The wounded animal had turned and overtaken his panic-stricken pony, taken its rider out of the saddle, and dashed him to the ground. Quite recently, he said, herds of elephant roamed in the broad valleys hereabouts, but had been driven westward by sportsmen. The spiky, pale-green leaves of the aloe plant, a favourite food of theirs, were to be seen here in abundance, and being in flower, its red and yellow blossoms lent a pleasing touch of colour to the sombre hue of the jungle.

Late in the afternoon we descended into the broad, darkly-wooded wadi lying on our left, along which we marched until sunset, when we encamped under some large trees on its banks. Right opposite to us lay the Hargaisa, on the slopes of the high ground beyond.

Hargaisa is one of the permanent settlements

in Somali-land, consisting of a large cluster of reed-mat huts, surrounded by a high thorn-fence. Whilst luxuriating in a wash in scanty attire in the open air, I had to receive the son of the principal "akal," or chief, of Hargaisa, with his following. The next morning I rode over to visit the head-man himself, Shaikh Mattar by name, whom I found a very pleasant old man. I was received with honour in his house, a large reed-mat structure, supported by forked props inside, with a dark interior. I had to go through an amount of hand-shaking with a crowd of Somalis, and then, after a little small-talk, obtained Shaikh Mattar's consent to my leaving a portion of my stores in his care until I should send back for them, as I was now near the Haud, and should soon require to load up some of my camels with water. On leaving I presented him with a couple of tobes of red, black, and white check, which are more costly, and considered more dressy than the everyday white tobe. The next day was spent in looking to my water-casks, which required soaking to render them water-tight. The "hāns"—large wicker-work baskets, vase-shaped, very cleverly made by the Somali women for carrying water—also required a little touching up. This a couple of women proceeded to do by rubbing in a mixture of ghee, and bark, and I do not know what else, which had the required effect, and also gave the water a most villainous flavour.

Early next morning we marched again for about three hours along the wadi, and then halted to fill up casks and hāns, for we were now approaching the Haud, and these were the last water holes we should meet with. So far things had not gone very well with me. I was minus the services of three camels, two having already terribly sore backs, and the other had had to be sent back sick almost at the start. Some of my men also complained of sickness. I poured a solution of carbolic acid into the holes in the backs of the former, and dosed the latter with quinine, and trusted to luck that they would come round.

We started again at noon, still keeping along the river bed, the jungle on either side excellent for tracking—good sandy soil, with tufts of grass. Mimosa and aloe grew everywhere, and also a bush of pale-green, fleshy stalks, very similar to whether I should get rain as I advanced farther in. Leaving the kāfila to pursue the track, I, with several of my men, walked through the jungle on one side. Game seemed plentiful. Soon I got glimpses of the red forms and long necks of the wary "gerenook" fleeing in the distance. After missing an oryx, I knocked over an unsophisticated "dhero" that stood to gaze, and soon after fired at the rump of another oryx grazing. A handsome male oryx dashed off at the shot at such a tremendous speed that I guessed he was hit. Hurrying forward on his tracks, we found splashes of blood, which we followed hard upon. But, although he was wounded badly, as the blood-splashes on grass and bush, upon which we followed all the way, showed, we must have tracked for a couple hours before we again saw him.

Suddenly we came on him, standing, with his flank exposed, looking back in our direction. I took a hurried shot, and the bullet was seen to strike the ground beyond him. "Na lagga" (missed), remarked Jama, looking very disgusted, and I felt so likewise, for the long march since the morning and the last two hours' continuous

## Lion-Hunting in Somali-land

the milk cactus of India, amongst whicl
favourite haunt of the lesser koodoo (*strc
imberbis*). From the number of pugs
koodoo and other game were plentiful,
soon came across one of the former sta
me over some bushes, and dropped him
bullet in the neck. He was a young ma
poor horns, but we all enjoyed him tha
for dinner.

The night of the following day fon
encamped at Fāff, a grassy "bān," o:
stretching to the horizon, within a few ]
yards of a Somali encampment near whic
made mine, hoping that lion would pay a
the night, for Somalis whom we had men
way told us of lion about here, and of l
had been encountered lying on the tracl
way of a passing kāfila.

We had marched early in the morning, (
a low ridge, and practically passing i
Haud. All about us rose a wall of ap]
interminable high bush jungle. The
was level, with no wadis, and as we pen
further the grass and bush had a par
appearance, causing me to feel anxiou:

tracking had taken it out of us. Fortunately, the oryx had been going much in the direction of our march, but we had very vague ideas as to where the kāfila was.

However, I could not give the beast up, so we again started on his tracks. Once we almost lost him, for his spoor became mingled with that of a herd of oryx, but, on following up the tracks of the herd we came to where the ground was much cut up by hoof-marks. "Larai kiya" (there has been a fight), grinned Jama, pointing to the ground. It was very evident that some of the herd, with that unnatural cruelty of animals to one of their own kind in misfortune had attacked and driven the wounded one out of their company. Following in the direction of the detached hoof-marks, we knew by traces of blood that we were going right, and before long we again sighted him, standing still with a dejected air, as if disgusted at the shabby behaviour of his own kind. It was a stern shot, so I aimed for his hind leg. He dashed off, but not far, for his hind leg swung in the air, and he came to bay under a tree. When we came up he snorted loudly, lowering his formidable horns, and looked so much like charging that we nearly fell over each other in our hurry to get out of his way. I was in want of meat for the men, and as the Somalis are strict Mahomedans, and will not eat the flesh of an animal that has not been "hallaled" (throat-cut) while living, it was necessary to cut the poor brute's throat. This was ticklish as well as unpleasant work, for the oryx made great play with his horns. At length, by breaking down strong, forked boughs, and entangling them in his horns with the assistance of the other men who had come up, we managed to throw him, and the necessary "halal" was carried out. My second shot, I found, was not altogether a miss, having passed through his neck.

With some difficulty we struck the track again, and, having examined the ground for fresh footmarks, were satisfied that the kāfila had not yet passed. So, pretty well fagged-out, we lay under the shade of a bush and took a nap until it made its appearance. Towards evening we got clear of the bush-jungle on to a wide plain covered with tussocks of grass, where, as I have said, we encamped. No lion paid us a visit during the night. Early next morning I went out into the plain to shoot something, and espied a red-looking animal in the distance, which turned out to be a hartebeest. After a long stalk in the open, I succeeded in bagging him, and returned to the camp laden with meat.

## CHAPTER II.

News had come in that a lion had visited a "karia" some few miles away, and had carried off a goat. I accordingly moved off there in the afternoon. I had walked on ahead of the kāfila, and was sitting on the ground waiting for it to come up, when a tall, picturesque-looking Somali in a red and black check tobe, with shield and spears, mounted on an unusually good-looking horse, rode up and greeted me. We got into conversation. He turned out to be a chief, the son of the "Sultan" of one of the tribes in whose country I was. Rain coming on just then he invited me and my kāfila to take shelter in his karia, which was close by. The next morning my new friend, whose name was Azkar, said he would like to join my party and show me where to get lions, since I had come to hunt in his country. I, of course, welcomed him, and a capital fellow he proved to be. Very soon all the karias scattered about the country knew that I had come to shoot lions, and was ready to give " bakshish" for good " khabar" (news) of them, and this was soon to have a good result.

I continued to move across the plain that day, halting in the evening at the edge of a belt of jungle, close to a karia where, the people said, lions constantly came at night. Recent spoor of lion close to where we were encamped showed that this was true enough. I tied up the two donkeys in different directions outside the zareba, but only some vile hyænas came and ate up one of them. The next day my rare good luck with the lions commenced. I had been out early into the jungle, shot an oryx, and succeeded in losing myself for a while. I got back to camp about midday rather fagged, and whilst at breakfast they came to tell me that a Somali had just ridden in with the news that two lions had been seen that morning out on the plain of Debīleh, lying outside a small bush, by one of the men of his karia. It was a long ride, they said, but, having heard the man's tale, it seemed good enough to chance it. My pony was saddled at once, and two animals hired from the karia for Jama and another Somali. Azkar also came with me.

It was quite two o'clock by the sun when we started, so we could not spare the ponies. We rode off at a brisk pace across the plain, which was dotted here and there with hartebeest, oryx, and gazelle, rarely drawing rein for the best part of eight miles, until we reached a karia where a very wild-looking Somali, the man who had seen the lions, joined us. From here we struck into a strip of low bush-jungle to our left, through which we rode at a fast pace for some little time, and then again emerged on to the grassy bān.

A great expanse of plain, reddish-brown in hue, and covered with tussocks of grass, stretched away as far as the eye could see. The sky had clouded over, and threatened rain. A delicious, cool breeze, with the freshness of rain in it, blew into our faces. Grazing herds of oryx, hartebeest, and gazelle were scattered over the plain, those nearer to us galloping away in alarm at our rapid approach, then wheeling round to stand and gaze at us at long rifle range. We continued to ride fast over the plain for another five or six miles, passing occasionally by black, withered thorn-fences, the disused Somali zarebas of previous years.

The pace at length began to tell on the animals. "How much further?" I asked anxiously, for the Abyssinian pony I rode began to show signs of exhaustion, and more than once nearly pitched me over her head, rifle and all, by floundering into some hole. The wild-looking Somali pointed to a small clump of bushes standing out against the sky-line some miles ahead. At last we drew near, and I could make out the bush more clearly. "Wā kā libah" (there are the lions), cried the Somali, just as I caught sight of two yellow animals lying outside it.

The absolute bliss of that moment is, of course, indescribable. Here had I two lions, actually waiting for me, all to myself, a vast plain on all sides, clear of jungle as a lawn, not another bush even in sight. I was going to get them—or they get me—that was the only uncertainty in the whole thing. Could the situation have been more perfect? Impossible. I regret now that I did not sit down and enjoy the full delight of it longer, but there was not much time, and I was in a hurry to commence. When we had ridden within a few hundred yards of the bush, I pulled up and told my party what they had got to do. Jama was to come with me, carrying the second gun, one man was to hold our horses, and Azkar and the other were to follow one or both lions should they run. Jama and I dismounted, and walked towards the bush. When we had approached within a hundred yards, the two lions, who had remained lying down all this time, rose—huge, yellow brutes they were, with black manes—and retired through the bush to the other side. I turned and took a look at Jama, who was behind me, for I had an unpleasant feeling that his gun, with triggers cocked, might be pointing at the small of my back. The triggers were cocked, in spite of my having told him not to do so, and it was quite within the range of probability, I saw, that he would either shoot at the lions before me or shoot me, neither of which I desired, so I stopped and gave him a bit of my mind, assuring him that if he fired at the lion, unless I was in difficulties, I would send him back to the coast, to which he was inclined to demur, saying something about the lion getting him, but I assured him that that was of no importance, and we went on, passing round by the right of the bush. When we had got round, there was a magnificent lion lying down not fifty yards away, looking towards us. I sat down promptly and fired at his shoulder. As the bullet struck him he leapt into the air, then stood uttering savage coughing roars at me. The majesty of the grand brute I shall never forget, as he stood there with his great jaws open breathing out his wrath. There was a grand, furious, indignant air about him that made one feel rather small, as being an unprovoked aggressor. His roars were nothing very tremendous, but his open, hanging jaws were most impressive.

In the meanwhile the other lion, which had lain down inside the bush, trotted out into the plain, and the two horsemen did not at first follow him. After yelling and waving frantically to them to do so I saw them ride off, and again turned my attention to my majestic friend. He still stood there snarling, but it was evident he was disabled. I fired again and, the shikari said, missed him. The grand brute then attempted to charge, but fell forward on to his head into the bush, where I killed him with a couple of shots from my second gun. Jama had remained close enough to me, but had disturbed me a good deal by calling out to me to fire in a very excitable way.

I did not stop then to look at my grand prize, but rushed off towards my pony, mounted, and galloped off in the direction the second lion had gone. Crossing over a slight rise I came upon the two horsemen motionless on the plain, and a couple of hundred yards from them I saw a yellow object lying on the ground—the lion, of course. I rode towards him, followed by Jama. When I had gone within one hundred yards of him the lion, who had been facing the horsemen, without moving his body now turned his head towards me, and received my approach with a show of teeth and much snarling. I pulled up and dismounted, though I was half inclined to fire at him from the saddle as Jama urged me to do, for the lion looked in an exceedingly nasty temper. Giving over my pony to one of the Somalis, I walked slowly towards the lion, bidding

Jama to remain in the saddle if he wished, but to keep as near as possible with the second gun. Very cautious and slow was my approach, for I did not want to bring on a charge before I had got in a shot, and it looked as if a too rapid advance would do so, for the lion, without stirring an inch, kept up a series of snarls and growls, giving me an excellent view of his teeth, accompanied all the while by short, sharp flicks of his tail on the ground. I walked up to within fifty yards of him, hoping to shoot him dead at that distance, and so avoid a charge. I then sat down and fired at him between the eyes, jumping to my feet instinctively to be ready if he charged. I was not a bit too soon. At the shot the lion sprang up with a furious roar. I had a lightning glimpse of him rearing up on his hind legs pawing the air—then he came for me. It was a fierce rush across the ground, no springing that I could see. How close he got before I fired I cannot say, but it was very close. I let him come on, aiming the muzzles of the rifle at his chest. Jama says he was about to spring when I pulled the trigger and ran back a pace or two to one side, but as I did so I saw through the smoke that the lion was stopped within a few paces of me.

The second gun and Jama were not as near as they might have been. The lion struggled up on to his hind quarters, uttering roars. I rammed two fresh cartridges into my rifle in an instant, and fired my right into him. The grand brute fell over dying. The Somalis set up a wild yell, and I am not sure that I did not join in. The lion looked dead enough, so I went up to him full of admiration of the grand brute. Of course, to me he was the finest lion, except his companion, that ever was shot; but in truth I had really got a prize. The mane was not remarkably long, but its colouring was particularly beautiful—a rich black on the shoulders, with bright, deep yellow on the head and cheeks. What a grand face it was. As I lifted the mighty forearms, it was impossible to escape a touch of regret for so noble a beast laid low.

It was with much interest I looked for the two bullet holes. My first shot had struck on the cheek-bone, smashing the left upper jaw, and knocking out the lower right canine tooth. It was evident from the result that I must have loaded my right barrel with a semi-hollow bullet, instead of a solid one of pure lead, there having been both kinds mixed together in my cartridge bag, though I had intended to use the latter only against lion. Fortunately for me, the left barrel contained a solid bullet. It had penetrated the chest, smashing the shoulder, and had raked along the flank, and, more important than all, had stopped, I believe by the very force of its impact, the lion's infuriated charge, which I consider the hollow bullet had let me in for. The rifle with which I killed all my lions was a Magnum 500 Express, by Tolley, firing 6 drams of powder. It proved itself a most trusty little weapon, and, with the pure-lead solid bullets, a great deal too much for lion. Leaving Jama to skin the lion, I rode off in haste to the first one, for I had altogether forgotten about the vultures, who might have been tearing his skin to pieces by this time. Fortunately, none had arrived on the scene yet. This was a magnificent lion. He looked a trifle bigger than his companion, and, judging by his teeth, was an old fellow.

His skull measures as follows:—Length, 14 inches; width, 10 inches; circumference, 25 inches, a half-inch broader and longer and one inch less in circumference than the skull of a big tiger. He had a remarkably beautiful mane, too—as regards its colouring—a pale yellow on the head, chest and cheeks, while on the shoulders, instead of the usual black, it was a rich brown, with a shade of red in it. That which struck me particularly on first seeing a lion in its wild state was that its loins and hind quarters had a proportional appearance of power with the rest of its body. There was none of that slack, weedy appearance behind which is so noticeable in the caged lion. I examined the bush where the lions had been lying-up, and, from the traces in it, it was evidently a regular resort of the pair, from which they no doubt went forth nightly to pull down their dinner from amongst the herds of antelope and gazelle, some of whom were still to be seen grazing at no great distance from the bush. I found the skull of a hartebeest close by, doubtless killed by them.

The sun was low, and a soft rain began to fall by the time we had got the skins off, with the great heads and paws intact, and tied them behind a couple of the horsemen, a no easy

MY FIRST LIONS. [p. 32.

matter, the ponies plunging and kicking with terror as they winded them. Off we went at last at a good pace, for we had to strike the track before dark. What a ride back that was over the breezy, rolling bān. I shall never forget the pleasure of it. What a paradise the country seemed, as my eyes wandered from the two great heads at the cruppers to the wild herds scattered over the plain. The Somalis, too, were very merry. As we rode the chief would break forth into impromptu song, in which, according to Jama's interpretation, he was very complimentary to me touching my encounter with the lions. Then one of the others would strike up a chant of his own, with more complimentary allusions to myself in particular, and Englishmen in general, and very much the reverse to Frenchmen and Italians, and so on.

When we reached the karia, where our guide had joined us, men, women, and children came flocking out from their zarebas to gaze at and touch the lions' heads, with much noisy exclamation. After the chief had made another sing-song oration from his saddle to the assembled Somalis, telling of the slaying of the lions, and I had done an amount of hand-shaking, we rode away along the track leading to camp. Night had fallen when we struck into the skirts of the jungle, where the gleam of my white tent and the welcome blaze of the camp fire showed up suddenly from out the gloom of the bush. Early next morning the Somalis of the neighbouring karias came crowding into my zareba to see the heads. According to many of them, the lions were a well-known pair in the neighbourhood. Pointing to the head of the larger lion, they said it was known as "Wadjha-ādad," or the white-headed one, and credited him with eating several persons. What truth there was in this I cannot say, but the colouring of the lion's head in question was strikingly fair in contrast to that of his fellow, and as to his man-eating propensities, man-eating lions are far from uncommon in Somali-land.

The following day we struck camp and moved on. We crossed the great red plain of Debīleh, with its herds of game, and passed the place where the lions had been. A headless skeleton was all that remained of the lion I had shot by the bush; feathers and claw-marks marked the ground. We were making for a dim, misty fringe of trees on the far horizon, seemingly in the mirage to be standing in the air out of a bank of mist. Clouds of dust here and there marked where troops of antelope careered over the plain, their forms assuming quaint shapes under the mirage effect. Not far from the bush a drenching thunderstorm came on. The camels began to slip and slide with their ungainly legs over the soaked earth threatening to topple over or split themselves, so a halt had to be called for the night.

Starting next morning, when the sun had dried the ground, we saw approaching us, from the direction we had come, long lines of camels, flanked by white lines of sheep and goats, driven forward by white-clad Somalis. Behind them came the usual string of camels, laden with the few household goods and reed mats which go to form a nomad Somali settlement. It was the large karia with which I had made acquaintance on the day with the lions, moving on into better pasturage ground. Late in the afternoon we reached the edge of a large tract of jungle, and encamped near a karia in the midst of a clump of freshly green mimosa trees. Here I stayed a few days, on the look out for lion, as the Somalis said that they had much frequented the place during the previous year's rainy season, harassing the different karias around with nightly raids after the cattle. Whilst the chief visited the nearer karias, and sent horsemen to the more distant ones, to learn news of lion, I had the most delightful antelope shooting imaginable.

## CHAPTER III.

In the early mornings, delicious with the freshness of the night's rain, I, with my two shikaris, would strike into the jungle behind our camp. All about us was green of the freshest hue; rich grass grew plentifully over the reddish-coloured earth, soaking our feet with the heavy dew or rain drops that lay upon it. In many spots blue, white, and yellow flowers grew in clusters. A wild maze of mimosa trees encircled us, their fantastic shapes and twisted branches lending a greater wildness to the scenery, whilst here and there the whitened skeleton of some ancient tree stood out in weird contrast to the living green of the jungle. Of the various wild life that roamed these wooded depths, the ground ever told its tale with the freshest signs. Spotted hyænas would get up close by us from out the grass, singly or in pairs, sometimes in a small troop, and go shambling off. However cautiously we might tread, the wary gerenook showed, by fleeing glimpses of their red forms, that they were too wide awake for us; the oryx, too, more easily detected by its larger bulk, would dash out at full speed from some clump of bushes, where he had stood unseen. Spoor of leopard, and once or twice of ostrich, were to be met with, but it was the lion's great paw-mark, broadly written on the soft earth, that sent a thrill through one; then it was that the spirit of the jungle took its strongest hold, drawing one farther and farther into its wild depths, ever looking to see the grim face in the gloom of some dense bush.

I had spent several days in these pleasant wilds, during which I had bagged four oryx, when news at last came from a distant karia that a lion had paid it a visit and carried off a sheep. As he was likely to repeat his raid, I moved my camp to the place. We marched all day through the tree jungle, where I had been hunting the oryx, and it was marvellous to me how the chief, who acted as guide, found his way through the labyrinth without a track or apparent landmarks. Towards evening we

"I HAD SPENT SEVERAL DAYS IN THESE PLEASANT WILDS." [*p.* 38.

arrived at the karia, where the people came out and showed me the lion's spoor in the soft earth outside the high thorn-fence, and the marks where he had dragged the animal along the ground for a short distance. The ground was too thickly covered with grass to allow of following up on the tracks if there had been time, so I decided to sit up for him over a live "kill" that night. After dinner I walked over from my camp, which was pitched at a short distance from the karia, to a low circular thorn-fence which my men had made outside the lofty zareba of the karia. Outside was the survivor of my donkeys, and when I arrived on the scene I found it had been attacked by a villainous hyæna during the few minutes it had taken Jama to tell me that all was ready. It was too dark to see what damage had been done, so I took up my post inside the low fence in company with Jama, who had armed himself with a long spear to retaliate on the hyæna, should he come for another mouthful. The night was black with rain clouds, and there was soon a heavy downpour. After an hour's sitting on the wet ground, with the rain dropping on to one, and the dim prospect of a lion turning up, it became more than I could stand, so I told Jama I was going. But it was not so easy to go, for the exit had been blocked up with heavy branches of the thorny mimosa, and it was no joke moving these in the dark. At last, when we emerged into the pitchy blackness of the jungle, Jama said he could not find his way back to camp. So I began to shout, and Jama joined in, to attract the notice of the Somalis inside the big zareba, but what with the bleatings of the sheep and goats, and the gruntings of the camels, we could not easily make ourselves heard. At last we managed to do that, and the reply we got was that no one cared about coming outside on such a dark night, with the lion probably prowling about; this accompanied with a good deal of laughter, which I felt was at our expense. Swearing having no effect, I began to offer bakshish through Jama, which, after a great deal of talking, had the desired result. Two Somalis, armed with spears, emerged, after taking their time about it. The donkey was untied, and we made our way back to camp, where our guides remained the night, not daring to return to their own zareba alone. The next morning I had to put a bullet into the poor donkey's head; the hyæna had wounded it terribly, taking a huge piece of flesh from between its thighs with one bite of its powerful jaws. I, of course, vowed I would never attempt night-shooting again, and did so again when the very first occasion offered itself.

The same morning I started out with Jama into the jungle to shoot something, disgusted with last night's performance, which had cost me a donkey. Less cautious than usual, I walked through the jungle talking with Jama, and I very soon paid the penalty for it. For our voices put up a couple of ostriches not over a hundred yards away from us; they went away like the wind, and had disappeared before I could even think of shooting. All through the day my ill-luck continued. Stalk after stalk did I do after oryx and gerenook, with the deplorable result of wounding two or three beasts which I never saw again. To put the finishing touch to it all, as I retraced my steps to camp, I came across a leopard slinking along through the bushes quite unconscious of me.

I ran quietly up to it to get within a hundred yards, fired and went over it. Sport appeared that day simply a vanity and vexation of spirit, and I continued my way back to camp in no amiable mood. A little further on Jama suddenly stopped and pointed. There was an oryx peacefully reclining in an open grassy space about a hundred and fifty yards away. I knelt and put a bullet into him. He went away as if it had merely invigorated him, and led me a pretty dance before I succeeded in bagging him. When I got back to camp there was the welcome news of lion awaiting me, and from this time an extraordinary run of good luck in encountering the king of beasts commenced for me.

Two mounted Somalis presented themselves and said they could show me a lioness with two cubs in a bush some miles away, if I would go with them at once. My pony was saddled, and I was off. We rode out of the bush across a grassy plain, where the going was excellent. It was a delicious ride, under a cool, cloudy afternoon sky, over the grassy level. Bad luck was soon forgotten, and sport was something considerably more than vexation. On the way the Somalis told me that in the night a lion had leapt over into their zareba and taken off a sheep; that the next morning they had followed on his spoor, and come on him lying close to a bush, with very little of the sheep left. He had got up, snarled at them, and walked slowly off. Looking into the bush they had seen two cubs, and taking it for granted that the lioness was also there, had made tracks. Having crossed the plain, we struck into some very thick bush jungle, and at last came in sight of the spot. The particular bush was exceedingly dense with closely interlaced branches—quite a wild beasts' lair. I dismounted and walked cautiously round it, with triggers cocked, unable to see into it, but fully expecting to hear the lioness growl, or see her rush out. Nothing of the kind occurred. So I went up to it, and peered in through its network of interlaced branches, and two of the dearest little faces, with dark-blue eyes, looked up at me from the inside. The cubs right enough, but where was the mother? There was not a sign of her. I was so much taken with the cubs that I was tempted to carry them off, but, of course, that would have been folly. Lion and lioness were sure to return during the night, I thought, so I decided to move camp into this jungle, and to pay the bush an early visit in the morning. The next day saw us riding briskly over the plain, and through the bush, bound for the lions' lair. A gallop across country in the delicious cool of the early morning is exhilarating enough in itself, as anybody knows, but when there is a probability of a shot at a lion at the end. Well, it is nearest to realizing the joy of living than anything I know of. However, it was not to come off just yet. No lioness sprang out to resent our approach to her home, but the cubs were still there—jolly little brownish-yellow fluffy creatures, no bigger than kittens, with the most quaintly solemn faces, upturned in wondering gaze at us peering in at them.

Neither lion nor lioness had been to the bush during the night, or the damp, bare ground around it would have told us so. I returned to camp and marched with the kāfila back into the neighbourhood of the bush, encamping within a mile of it. As the kāfila moved slowly across the open plain, I took my rifle and went off with Jama after a herd of hartebeest. Looking as unconcerned as possible, we gradually approached the herd, as if we intended to pass round, but edging towards them. Coming to a small bush I dropped to the ground behind it, while Jama went on assuming an air of great innocence, and now inclining away from them. The beguiled hartebeest continued to stare at Jama's retreating figure, while I took the opportunity to crawl towards another small bush within easier range. But they caught sight of me before I could gain it and began to trot off. Luckily a buck, with a handsome dark-red skin, was inquisitive enough to stand and gaze at the object which had cropped up so suddenly; his curiosity proved fatal to him. I sat up and took a full head on him behind the shoulder, judging the distance at about two hundred yards. The next moment he lay kicking on his back, and the rest of the herd were in full flight. I ran up to the fallen hartebeest, and found the bullet had gone high, breaking his back near the withers. It was a welcome supply of fresh meat for camp.

We pitched our camp near the karia from which the lion had taken the sheep. The people said that the lion had been roaring near them in the night, and showed me where he had left some of his mane on the high, double thorn-fences of their zareba, which I should say were at least twelve to fourteen feet high, with a space of two or three yards between the inner and outer walls. A no small feat to get over such a fence and carry off a sheep back by the same way, not to speak of the fearless audacity in leaping into the midst of a zareba crowded with Somalis and animals, for I can imagine the hulla-balloo that would greet the lion's daring descent would be something appalling. Well, the next morning we again paid a visit to the bush, with a similar result; so I decided to sit up over a donkey near the bush that night, in hopes of getting the lion. My shikaris spent the day in building a small circular fence, about six feet high, near the bush. A little before sunset I took up my rifle and set out to pass the night in the jungle. Both the shikaris came with me, one carrying blankets, the other dragging an unwilling, aged donkey, for which I had had to pay a fancy price to a hard, bargaining Somal.

The jungle about the lion's home was rather dense, though the bush itself stood in a small patch of open ground. Some twenty yards away was my zareba, so cleverly constructed that I did not at once distinguish it from the surrounding jungle. We, of course, investigated the bush first. The cubs were still there, seeming such helpless little creatures to be out in the wilds alone. The donkey is tied up outside, close to the hole in the fence through which I should fire. Alas! that I never looked to see how, for thereby hangs the tale. We crawled inside, shut up the entrances with a heavy branch, spread our blankets, and waited. The jungle soon grew dark; black clouds, which I had noticed gathering on the horizon, spread over our heads, shutting out all light from the sky, and heavy drops of rain soon began to fall. After we had lain some time in weary wakefulness without speaking, Jama started up, laying his hand on my arm. I raised my head, and through the intense silence of the jungle came a far-away, deep, moaning sound. Jama's grasp tightened.

I understood. It was the lion's roar. I listened for it again, every nerve tingling with the pleasure of intense expectation. After a long interval, again and again the sullen sound broke the silence more loudly, dying away in the same moaning note. Then an apparently interminable time elapsed, during which I sat up straining my ears, very fearful that he might not be coming near us after all. A creepy silence reigned. Suddenly there was a soft sound of the heavy brute's gallop over the ground outside, a crash and thud as the donkey was felled to the ground, while his bray rang out piteously in the night air. A slight noise of struggle, a few more stifled brays, and then stillness, save for the lion's heavy breathing a few feet from us. Under cover of the noise I had cocked my triggers, fearful lest their clicking might be heard, and now peered out through the hole but nothing but an indistinguishable dark mass could I make out in the pitchy darkness. So I waited. After tugging at the donkey and finding he could not drag it away, the lion began his meal. There was a crunching of jaws and a tearing of flesh, and then, with a loud, cracking sound, the animal's ribs were torn asunder with one most mighty wrench. All this was accompanied by a loud purring sound, then followed a gurgling, lapping noise as the lion drank up the blood in the donkey's stomach. After this he renewed his efforts to drag away the carcase, and Jama excitedly whispered to me to fire. I again peered out, but could simply see nothing of the lion, so black was the night, although the tugging went on all the time. It seemed folly to risk a shot, and I determined to wait for dawn if necessary, fondly believing that the donkey was properly secured. Just then the lion gave a great heave, and, to my unspeakable disgust, I heard the carcase being dragged away. I glared out through the hole in desperation, but it was now hopeless to attempt a shot. I could see nothing, though I heard him taking a few more mouthfuls not many yards away. Then the dragging noise commenced again, until it died away in the bush—lion and donkey were gone.

Then I inquired and learnt that the end of the rope to which the donkey was fastened had been put in the hole in the ground, and the earth tamped round it. I blessed Jama profusely, and then got to sleep the best way I could, intending to follow up the tracks at daybreak, in the hope of stealing on the lion as he lay by the carcase. So, in the gray dawn, we crawled out of our shelter, and stole quietly on the broad trail, which the dragging of the body had made over the grass. We had not proceeded far when the remains of the donkey, under a bush, came in sight, and almost at the same moment I had a view of a massive-looking lion, with a good mane, trotting slowly away through the jungle. The bushes hid him before I could get in a shot, and though I ran hard after him, the jungle was so thick that he escaped me; nor did the grass-covered soil allow us to follow him up. Disconsolately we dragged back the donkey to where it had passed the night, and returned to camp, wondering where on earth the lioness could be. The same day my men went out and secured each of the donkey's legs to stakes driven into the ground, close up against the fire-hole of my zareba, for I decided to sit up again that night, thinking the lion was pretty sure to return to his kill. However, news came in of lion, which some Somalis had seen in a plain a long way off. It resulted in a tremendous long ride, and my seeing nothing. I came back to camp, dead beat, late in the evening, and not inclined to sit up that night for all the lions in Africa. Sorely was I punished for my slackness, for when we paid our early visit to the spot next morning, there, all about the bush, were the fresh big "pugs" of the lion, and, at last, those of the lioness too. The donkey was gone, each rope had been bitten through, and the lion's great paw-marks close to our zareba showed he must have stood with his head or chest close up against the hole through which I should have fired.

We again followed on the trail of the donkey, and had gone about a mile when we espied the very small portion that remained of it in a dense thicket. The lion was not there, and we had now only his spoor to follow over the close grass, which the heavy rain of the night just enabled us to do very slowly. Suddenly I, being mounted, saw ahead of the trackers, beyond the surrounding bush, the great brute's yellow body. He was trotting off, evidently disturbed. I dashed after him, but was soon brought to a standstill, mixed up with a bush. The other horsemen also failed to keep him in view, and I never saw the lion again.

We returned to the bush—the cubs were gone,

and the lioness's spoor led away into the jungle in another direction. I suggested to follow them up, but Jama said it was useless. A very good fellow, however, a head-man of the neighbouring karia, named Ibrahim, volunteered to try and send me back word if he should track the lioness down. The sun was hot, and I was hungry and lazy enough to consent; so, while he and a friend followed on the spoor, the rest of us returned to camp. As I was in the middle of breakfast, his companion rushed into my tent in a state of great excitement. His story was that, after they had taken up the spoor some little distance, the lioness had suddenly sprung out from a thick bush and stood snarling at them in front of it. They had speedily withdrawn, and now Ibrahim was watching over the place at a distance while he had come in with the news. Ponies were obtained at once for my shikari and messenger, and I pushed through the jungle as fast as possible, but I had soon to put a curb on my impatience, for the man lost his way—and in such a maze of bush it was no wonder. From a walk it came to dismounting and casting about for foot-marks. At last we struck on these, and as we slowly followed on them, there came a low whistle from out the surrounding bush. Looking about us we saw Ibrahim kneeling under a tree—his attitude was striking—he held his spear at the charge, and in the other hand his long Somali knife. He pointed to a bush some sixty yards away, to intimate where the lioness was. I looked hard, and behind a fallen tree, which lay in front of the entrance to the bush, I saw the yellow head of the crouching lioness. I had had enough of head shots since my last experience, so, cocking my triggers, I walked slowly towards the lioness, intending to shoot when I could see something more of her. I had approached within about twenty paces of her when she sprang up and over the trunk, with two short, coughing roars. Thinking she was coming for me I stopped and threw up my rifle to fire. She did not charge, however, but stood there snarling, on guard, as it were, over her lair, and a big, yellow beauty she looked. She did not face me exactly, but stood with head turned to one side, as if looking at me out of the corner of her eye, and giving me a side view of her teeth. It was very much the position which I understood Mr.

Selous to say in his first book is believed by the Dutch hunters to denote an intention to charge. Whatever her meaning was, I wasted no more time in shooting at her. I sat down promptly and fired at her left shoulder, which she thus exposed to me. With a furious roar she sprang up in the air, and seemed to fly back through her lair. I jumped up and fired the left barrel as she disappeared through the bushes, very nearly blowing out the brains of the guide, who had rushed forward almost in front of the rifle to see what had happened. Very cautiously we followed through the bushes where she had gone, but had not proceeded far before we saw her stretched under a thicket, gasping out her life. She was quite done for, and I was able to handle her while she still breathed. What a powerful, sleek beauty she looked! What mighty muscles lay beneath that yellow, glossy skin of hers! I could not admire her enough. Jama, however, began to skin, so I went off to the bush, and there were the little cubs again, looking much disturbed, and there was much fierce infantile growling, accompanied with bites and scratches for the hands that took them prisoners. They

A LION ON THE PROWL. [p. 55.

were male and female, and the little lion showed his masculine superiority of spirit by remaining wilful and bad-tempered long after his sister had settled down quietly.

Ibrahim's behaviour in this affair was very plucky. He told me that the lioness had come out of the bush more than once and snarlingly threatened him. To have stood his ground under such circumstances for a good hour until I arrived, with only a spear and knife to defend himself, showed great pluck, I consider. My little captives became inmates of my tent, and afforded me much amusement in watching their little lion-like ways. It seemed so absurd that such soft, fluffy-haired little creatures could ever develop into the mighty king of beasts. And yet the traces were all there. In their solemn little faces you saw the lion's grand head. In the stealthy manner they moved you saw his prowling gait. As evening fell they loved to prowl forth out of my tent into the darkness at the end of their long ropes, calling to each other with most diminutive cries. They would eye the very milch-goat that was obtained to suckle them, as if about to do a stalk on it, eliciting shouts of laughter from my men, who would crowd round to see the lions fed. Suckling them became almost an impossibility, for they would claw the poor goat so in her tenderest parts, so that one day I tried them with chopped-up raw antelope-meat, and, to my surprise, the precocious little creatures devoured it ravenously. It seemed remarkable that the lioness should have left them for four days: I can be pretty well positive that she never visited them for that time, for otherwise her spoor would have been found in the soft soil round the bush. Did the lion, then, feed the cubs on meat during her absence? It seems probable, from the kindly way they took to raw flesh; yet they could not have been many weeks old.

"PLUCKY IBRAHIM AND CUBS."

## CHAPTER IV.

I WAITED a few days in hopes of getting their father, but nothing more was heard or seen of him. I then marched in the same direction that I had ridden on the long, wild-goose chase for lion, whereby I had lost the lion and lioness the same night, over the kill, and encamped in some jungle not far from a vast bān and a range of mountains. Here I remained for the rest of my leave, meeting with such a run of good luck with lion that I could not tear myself away from the spot, although I got the tempting "khabar" of man-eating lion, and also rhinoceros, not more than a day's march or so from where I was. The day following my arrival I went out, in company with the chief and four other mounted Somalis, to hunt for lion.

We rode through the skirts of the bush-jungle down on to a rolling, grassy plain stretching away to the far distance. To our left ran the rugged range of the Harrar mountains, with a dark, broad belt of dense forest lying along its base. Ahead of us, on the horizon, the few isolated peaks of Jīga-Jīga rose abruptly against the blue background of sky. Far away to the right Jīfa-Ūri and several other peaks raised their pointed heads above the line of the horizon. Elsewhere the eye rested on a huge, sun-dried, grassy expanse alone, save where a small, conical hill stood out a conspicuous landmark in its midst: a true African landscape in all its mighty vastness.

Riding was most enjoyable, for the morning was cool and breezy, with a cloudy sky. My Somali friends were in high spirits; one or other of them would dash to the front at full speed on their sturdy little ponies, to display their horsemanship, then bring up their animals almost on to their haunches at a dead halt, and stabbing in the air with their spears. This must have been very poor fun for the ponies, for they are most cruelly bitted, poor beasts! and their mouths were often covered with blood and foam. So we rode on, laughing, chatting, or breaking into song, down into the great plain towards the belt of forest at the foot of the mountains. At length we drew near to a patch of open tree-jungle, which jutted out into the plain, and I told Azkar to get the horsemen to spread out in couples.

We had not ridden far into the jungle, when I saw Azkar riding fast between the tree-trunks towards me. He brought the joyful news that they had come upon fresh spoor of lion, which his companion was following up. I rode with him to the spot. There were the paw-marks, freshly imprinted in the rain-soaked earth. In hot haste we followed on them, and soon came up with the Somali, who had gone on, at a standstill. The few words, in a low, excited tone, he spoke to Azkar needed no interpreting to tell me that the lions were close at hand. I was out of the saddle in an instant, and walking towards a thicket pointed out to me, while they rode to one side, to get round the bush and cut off the lions' retreat. At first I saw nothing, but, as I approached, I made out two large, yellow animals inside the thicket, and some cubs. They were evidently disturbed, looking in the direction the horsemen had ridden, and not noticing me. Suddenly a fine-looking lioness sprang out and cantered off slowly. The other, also a lioness, stood looking about, evidently the mother of the cubs, from her reluctance to leave. I got down at once, and aimed at her about fifty yards distant. As I fired she moved out of the bush, and then she sprang away in the direction of the horsemen, and disappeared, leaving me uncertain whether I had hit.

I sent off the Somali who carried my second gun to bring up my pony, and ran hard after her. Just when I was thoroughly out of breath I came upon her, sitting up on her haunches under a large tree, looking very angrily at the Somalis, who stood hooting at her from a respectful distance. When I appeared on the scene she turned her head towards me, and a splendid yellow brute she looked as she sat there. I walked slowly towards her, trying to recover my wind, and when within about fifty yards I fired. Without appearing to feel the shot, she charged at once across the open ground that lay between us. I stood up and waited for her, keeping the muzzles pointed below her mouth as well as I could. I had time to notice that she seemed somewhat disabled in the hind quarters, and that her charge was slow compared with the pace at which the lion had come on; also to remember that my second gun was nowhere near. I let her come on to within a dozen yards, then fired. The smoke hung hiding everything for the moment. "Has she got me?" was the thought that flashed through me as I stepped aside. No—there she was, staggering back on her haunches, with jaws wide open, covered with blood, not many paces away. Stepping back as I reload, I gave her a bullet in the side, to which she fell over and died. My pony arriving on the scene, the whole of us dashed off through the trees in search of the second lioness, and very soon came upon her standing under a tree. She sprang away at a gallop on seeing us, and we followed hard after. It was a magnificent sight to see the great yellow brute bounding between the tree-trunks of the open jungle with long, easy strides, and had it not been that I was afraid of losing her in the closer jungle for which she was making, I would have enjoyed the gallop behind her for a good deal longer. Finding herself being overtaken, she stopped abruptly under a tall tree, and faced us. We also pulled up with advisable expedition.

How clearly I can see it all as I recall the scene—the tall trunks of the park-like jungle surrounding us, the lioness standing at bay beneath a tree, looking grandly savage, her head held low, with jaws open, breathing savage snarls, her forelegs set wide apart. Slowly, to and fro, she sways, her thick tail held straight out in the air, as stiff as any iron bar. Her temper is up, and she means fighting in every inch of her.

I have dismounted, and am walking towards her with rifle cocked, while the Somali horsemen ride to get round her, and her glance travels to and fro between us. She looked such a devil that I had no particular desire to go nearer than need be, so, when within sixty or seventy paces, I knelt and fired. She charged on the instant, apparently untouched. I thought she was coming for me at first, but was by no means sorry to see her swerve off after the horsemen. The speedy way the whole group turned tail and fled in hot haste, with the lioness making her furious rush behind them, was most amusing.

Reloading my right barrel as I went, I ran after the lioness, disappearing amongst the trees. I very soon came up with her again, standing in the open, not far off, looking about her. The Somalis had cleared out of sight. She stood looking about her, lashing her tail to and fro in a very earnest kind of manner. Further I did not study her appearance, but got down and fired again pretty quickly, and was very well pleased to see her fall over to the shot. I walked up as she rolled about, making furious efforts to get up, and had to put two more bullets into her before she died. My first shot was a very bad one, hitting her far back, and doing little damage. The other lioness turned out to be the mother of the cubs, for her teats had milk in them. The shot which had stopped her charge had struck her in the mouth, carrying away most of the lower teeth in front, and had then pierced her throat. The cubs were not to be found when we turned to look for them, but we did not search far, hoping to find them with their father the next day, for I supposed there must be a male lion somewhere close at hand.

The following day a party of us rode to the spot, and found the cubs in the bush where the lionesses had been, but there were no signs of a lion. The cubs were much bigger than those I had got, and were extremely savage and valiant little creatures. Such fierce pretences of charging out on us did they make, accompanied with so much furious growling, that our ponies began to dance about in fright. It seemed such a pity to take the jolly little animals away from a life of freedom in the jungle, to existence in a cage, that I decided to leave them for a few days to see if they could shift for themselves. It ended, however, in my taking them, for the Somalis said they would kill them if I did not.

I had now quite a menagerie, and my camp was never free from Somalis, especially women and children, peering over the zareba, to have a look at the young lions. The new-comers were so savage that I had to keep them separate from the little ones. At first they would not eat even the freshest raw meat, and the male soon died; but the female at length took to her food, but remained unapproachable, until one day Jama brought the two little cubs to where she was lying. The savage little animal became transformed. The delight with which she welcomed the small strangers of her own race, rolling over on her back, as if to play with them, purring loudly, uttering cries of delight, and caressing them with licks was a pretty and touching sight to see. So they were left together, and a very happy family they were while in camp, and the big female cub became so tame that she would allow me to take her up on my knee—that is so long as a little one was also taken up with her, but separate them and she was a fury once more.

The following morning saw us in the saddle again. More mounted Somalis joined me this time, volunteering to help in the search for lion. Our luck with the lionesses, and the consequent bestowal of bakshish on the fortunate few with me, being the attraction that drew.

So we were a large party as we rode down the grassy slopes towards the plain. And a picturesque group they made, these lean, wild-looking horsemen of the Habr-Āwal tribe, as they rode, bare-legged, their tough little ponies, that plunged to the slightest touch on the cruel bits; white tobes flying in the wind, spears bristling, quaint saddlery, adorned with red woollen tufts, quainter stirrups, admitting of the rider's big toe alone, and impressing you with the muscular power of that member in the Somal, for so he will ride all day. And a very merry crew they were, too, singing and laughing, racing pony against pony, or dashing to the front at headlong speed, then curbing in on the instant to spear an imaginary foe. But this was not business, and it required much exhortation through Azkar before I could get them to scatter over the country in couples. In this way we swept along the edge of the jungle at the foot of the mountains, where the going was good, through long grass and widely-growing clumps of bush and tree. Startled oryx and gazelle galloped away from us at every turn, and now it would be a long line of ostriches scudding away like the wind towards the open. Suddenly I see Azkar riding fast between the bushes, chasing something. I spurred hard towards him, and, as I come up, I see something yellow flashing through the grass. What on earth is it,

I wonder? And Azkar shouts out "Shebeyle." A leopard I think, and congratulate myself on being in for some more fun. Just then the animal came to bay, crouching out of sight in the long grass. I dismounted and fired into the patch where it was crouched. A vision of claws, teeth, and yellow fur sprang into the air then subsided. I walked up cautiously, and, to my disgust, found that all is not leopard that answers to the name "shebeyle." I put it down to be a very large tiger-cat. It had a bright yellow skin, with black spots widely placed. All the Somalis called it "shebeyle," but when Jama, who was of the low-caste, hunter-tribe of "Midgāns," saw it, he smiled a contemptuous smile at them, and called it "aramāt," saying it was destructive to sheep and goats. It was about the size of an English fox, I should say. We continued our search along the border of the jungle, finding a lion's tracks, which we did not succeed in taking up far, and riding down within easy distance of the rugged peaks of Jīga-Jīga on the western horizon, near which was an Abyssinian outpost, marking the line of invasion of the Gallas. For this reason the country in which I was hunting was much avoided by the Somalis, although it afforded excellent pasturage in the rainy season, owing to the aggressiveness of the rifle-armed Abyssinian, to oppose whom the Somalis are at a great disadvantage with their spears. Many were the complaints I heard on this head from the Somalis, who would point out that the "Sir-kāl" (here meaning British Government) will neither allow rifles to be imported, nor help them against the Abyssinians.

## CHAPTER V.

ONE morning I was taking my ease inside my tent after breakfast, with every intention of doing a thorough loaf in camp, when two Somali boys came in with a tale of how they had been loitering about the spot where I had shot the pair of lionesses, when a lion's growl in the bushes close by had caused them to quit hurriedly. Their story became very vague on questioning them, but still I thought it worth while to go and see, and was just riding off with a few Somalis to the spot, when a horseman galloped up to the zareba with the delightful news that there was a lion marked down for me. He said that during the night a lion had been roaring round his karia; that, early next morning, he and two others had ridden out to look for him, and had met with his majesty walking out on the great bān, far from any jungle, who, on finding himself followed, had crouched in the grass, and that there he was now, with two mounted Somalis watching over him. This sounded a much better story, and we at once galloped off to interview the lion. As we rode, details of his appearance were interpreted to me. There never was such another lion—with such a mane—before.

After a very pleasant, brisk ride through the bush, past several karias and their herds of grazing camels, goats, and sheep, we emerged on to another part of the great plain I have already described. Then a gallop of a mile or two over its undulating, grassy slopes, and we sighted the figures of a couple of horsemen standing out on the plain. As we drew close to them, the Somalis pointed out what appeared to me a small, brown bush appearing above the sea of waving grass—it was the lion's head. I dismounted, and proceeded to walk him up. The big, brown, hairy head still stuck up above the grass, taking us all in, and I was just thinking that I should like to see more before I shot, when the lion ducked his head, and left me nothing to gaze at but the waving grass of the plain. This was a wily move on his part, and I stood puzzled, thinking it out. The grass between us was rather long, reaching above my knees. He had disappeared in a small patch of somewhat taller grass, which helped me to mark where he lay. If I fired into that patch I should probably hit him, but the chances were that I would merely wound him, and then a charge was a pretty dead certainty. Somewhat of a toss-up at any time, it seemed less desirable just then, as I considered the difficulty in keeping aim on the animal, as it charged through the long grass.

Not seeing my way out of the situation standing where I was, I advanced slowly, trusting that that rush through the grass would not come off, until I had got in a shot.

At last, when some forty yards off, I espied a vague, small, brown patch in the grass where I had marked the lion down—what part of him, it was impossible to say—so I went on and on, until I was within twenty paces of the lion. Still I could see no more of him, and still the lion gave no sign—nothing but the wind sweeping over the plain moved the grass where he lay. Unknowing, one would have walked right on to him. I had gone far enough now I considered, for the silent, crouching brute in the grass inspired one with caution, so back I stepped, very slowly, lest I might draw him on to me, until I had doubled the distance between us. Then I called out to the Somalis to throw stones on to him. Azkar and another rode up to me and did so, and they all began to hoot at him, but these indignities failed to draw our wily friend in the grass to show himself in the slightest; so, having no more patience left, I decided to shoot, and risk the result. The lion lay exactly forty paces, as I afterwards measured, from where I stood. I took as steady an aim, as I could standing, at the brown patch, just distinguishable at that distance. The breeze carried the smoke of my rifle clear of my front at once, so it was almost simultaneously with the crack of the rifle that I saw great paws and a tail appear above the grass. There were deep, gurgling snarls, accompanied with a tremendous commotion in the grass, but nothing charged out of it. So, after waiting a little while, I walked into the patch, and there, amidst the crushed down-grass, lay a full-grown, black-maned lion struggling in his death throes.

I put another bullet into him to end his sufferings, and the mighty brute lay stretched out dead before me. My first shot, a pure-lead, solid bullet, had struck under the left eye in almost exactly the same place where I had hit the second lion with a hollow bullet, who had charged, but with how different a result. On skinning we found it had penetrated through skull and neck into his chest, practically killing him.

The next few days I spent with the oryx, and had one or two interesting experiences. I had been so much taken up lately with riding about the country looking for lion that we found ourselves without meat in the larder. So I sallied out with my shikaris one morning to supply the want. Of course, with the usual perverseness of things in general, game made itself scarce, and I could not get a shot at anything for some hours. At length an oryx did turn up, and I put a bullet into him, only to send him off apparently more vigorous than ever. We followed, but never saw him again. So, on we tramped wearily, under a midday sun, I vowing I would not return without meat. At last we came out on to an open, grassy space, and espied an oryx, right out in the very midst of it, grazing. There was nothing but grass all around him for many hundreds of yards—not a bush, not an anthill—nothing to screen our approach. How were we going to get him? It looked impossible. We sat down to talk it over, but did not see our way any the better for that, so we continued to sit and look, coveting the oryx's flesh, when, lo and behold! greatly to our joy, the oryx himself sits down with his back to us. Now, there was a chance for us, and Jama and I at once got down on our stomachs and dragged ourselves over the ground as best we could, the grass—which was not very long—our only cover. We scarcely dared to raise our heads to see if the oryx was still there. Jama could wriggle himself along like any snake, as if to the manner born, and would turn his head and grin back at me, as I came, slowly and laboriously, after him, more than once having to lie on my face, utterly blown, gasping for wind. An occasional peep above the grass showed us the oryx nodding in blissful unconsciousness. At length we succeeded in getting within about 150 yards, when I took a very shaky shot at him, and was much disgusted to see him get up and go away in a great hurry. Jama said he heard the bullet tell, so we followed, and a pretty dance he led us. Several times I had crawled up to him, and would be just raising myself out of the grass to fire when he would see me and be off. At last the oryx got to the edge of some tree-jungle, where he stopped the further side of a bush. Now, I thought, I had him, and, vowing I would take him back as meat to camp, I commenced another crawl. In the middle of it Jama touched my arm. I looked up and saw a fine cock ostrich, with plenty of black plumage about him, followed by another, come running across our front, within easy shot. But even this rare chance failed to tempt me to forego my shot at the oryx, so bent was I on getting him after the trouble he had given. But the sacrifice was in vain, for the oryx escaped me after all, and I returned to camp late in the afternoon haunted by that ostrich's curly black plumes, which might have been mine. When the ostriches ran past us we saw a "Midgān," armed with bow and arrow, a veritable wild man of the woods, come out from behind some bushes and pick up an arrow which he had fired at them. We had evidently both been stalking our game at the same time. A day or two after this we had meat in plenty. We were hunting in some very pretty jungle of long, green grass, sprinkled with flowers and umbrella-shaped mimosa trees, when we sighted a large herd of oryx scattered amongst the bushes ahead of us. Stalking a herd scattered in this way is no easy matter, for the females are numerous and very watchful, and often spoil one's little game by giving the alarm from an unexpected quarter. As we crept towards them stealthily from bush to bush, suddenly the whole herd began to move in our direction. Jama hurried me off under the shade of a tree by which they must pass quite closely. The tree afforded no cover, and as we squatted under it, it seemed to me that we could not have chosen a worse position. But Jama said that as long as we did not move the herd would pass by without seeing us, and it was evident he understood their ways. For, sure enough, the whole herd came trooping by us not 20 yards off, and a prettier sight of that kind I have not seen. Their greyish, roan-coloured bodies, barred with black, took a pinkish hue in the bright sunlight, as they glanced through the green foliage. A stately looking oryx, arching its neck and showing a fine length of horns, led the way; behind came the crowd, with many young ones gambolling by their mothers' sides. Feeling very murderous as I did so, I covered the leader and fired. It fell to the shot instantly, and never stirred, while the whole herd, after a panic-stricken pause, dashed off in all directions in wild alarm, not, however, before I had emptied the left barrel into what I took to be another male, and brought it kicking to the ground in a cloud of dust. It was up again, however, the next moment and away. Having "hallāled" the first, which, much to my regret, I found was a female, we went after the other, and eventually bagged it, it being also a female. With oryx this mistake is more excusable, for the females have often longer, although slightly thinner horns than the male, and not only I, but also my shikari, failed to distinguish the sex.

Towards evening of the same day a Somali came into camp to say that he had that afternoon seen four lions out in the bān. So the next morning I went off, under his guidance, in company with Azkar and several other Somalis, on the chance of finding traces of them, but with no success. As we continued to ride over the plain, we sighted a party of Somalis travelling from the direction of Harrar, in the Galla country, and my gossip-loving companions galloped off to interview the strangers and learn the news. They had much to say against the Abyssinians, who now hold Harrar, and also stared at me with curious eyes; and, doubtless, I cut a queer enough figure in my blue sun-glasses, battered shikar-topee, and dirty brown shooting-kit.

Leaving these people, we were riding for the distant line of jungle stretching along the foot of the mountains, when Azkar suggested sending horsemen to reconnoitre the little conical hill which stood out so conspicuously on the plain, where lion, he said, were sometimes known to make their haunt in the few bushes growing on its bare sides. I welcomed the idea, for I was lazily inclined. There was a broiling hot sun overhead that day, and the great bān seemed to throb and quiver under its fiery rays, and in the shimmering heat the little bare hill seemed very far away. So two Somalis rode off, while we stretched ourselves out in the long, dry grass to bake in the hot sunshine, with our hobbled ponies grazing alongside, and await their return.

After a long wait, one of the horsemen appeared in sight, returning at a gallop. This must mean something unusual. Could it be lions? Such luck again so soon seemed scarcely possible. Such were my thoughts as, in hot haste, I saddled my pony and rode to meet the man, followed by the others. Let the reader imagine, if he be a shikari, what his own joy would have been when the man cried out "Libah!" (lions), and held up four fingers. We rode on to the hill together at a fast pace. As we drew near, the ground became very stony, and assumed an extremely burnt-up appearance, with tall, yellow, waving grass growing all about it. Having ridden half round the hill, we came upon the lions. The first thing I saw were two yellow heads sticking up above the grass; then, as I proceeded to walk these up, three young lions, about three-parts grown, bounded off for a short distance, and then again crouched. As I was about to follow after them, Jama called out to me to shoot the big one, and, on turning round, I perceived, for the first time, a full-grown lioness sitting up in the long grass quite close to me. I fired at her at once; upon which she made a dash at Azkar, who was riding near, but failed to catch him. When she stopped, I again fired and knocked her over. I then went after the young lions, who gave me a great deal more trouble. Each one, as I walked him up, made a short charge at me through the grass, accompanied by a formidable amount of noise—a deep grunting or roaring, for it is hard to define the noise a lion makes on charging. But they did not come on, except one, which I believe would have if I had not given him a bullet. It turned out there were five, but I never saw the fifth; it must have got away unseen in the long grass. The rapidity with which numbers of great vultures gathered to the spot was astonishing. I had not noticed a sign of them in the hot, blue heavens, and yet the last lion had scarcely been shot, when they were hovering over our heads, or swooping boldly down towards the dead lions. As we abandoned each carcase to their ravenous maws, after removing the skin, the hideous birds would come flocking to it, half-running, half-flying along the ground, their bald, fleshy necks outstretched; and soon the carcase was hid from view by a moving, dark-feathered mass of bodies, above which their bare heads and snaky necks bobbed up and down as they jostled and tore at the flesh, and marvellously soon nothing but a black-looking skeleton remained. As I stood and looked on, strangely fascinated, at a mass of vultures gathered over the carcase of the lioness, quite undisturbed by my near presence, I thought how typical a picture it was of the wilds of Africa. Except where, in the far distance to the south, ran the blue-grey line of the jungle-girt mountains of Harrar, bordering the great bān, the huge landscape of plain stretched away on all sides to the horizon, where in one direction the mirage threw a dim fringe of trees into the sky. Over its vast sea of withered grass the heated atmosphere seemed to run in dancing, quivering lines under the fierce sunshine. In the foreground squatted my wild-looking companions, their spears stuck upright in the ground, their hobbled ponies grazing near. Above us rose the bare little conical hill; in the hot, cloudless blue overhead the birds of death were hovering or swooping down towards the freshly-skinned carcase of a lion. Over all the yellow glare, and the sough of a sudden, welcome breeze in the long, dry grass.

## CHAPTER VI.

AND now I come to the reddest of red-letter days in my shooting reminiscences. I had set out early one morning with Azkar, Jama, and four other Somalis, to search the country for lion. We rode westward, keeping inside the edge of the bush, where the dark tract of jungle, stretching along the foot of the mountain range, met the grassy bān. By noon we had covered a great deal of ground, seeing numbers of oryx and Soemmering's gazelle, ostrich occasionally, and bustard everywhere—but no lion. Then, penetrating deeper into the forest jungle, we struck upon a delightfully refreshing and picturesque spot—a shallow water-channel, thickly carpeted with luxuriant grass, where abundance of rain-water stood in tempting pools, surrounded by green thickets of bush and trees. Here we rested and watered our ponies, while my Somalis took the opportunity to wash themselves and their clothes, a rare luxury in the Haud. In the night lions had come here to drink, for we found their great paws deeply scored in the soft earth round the pools. On following them up, we were led into the track of a whole troop of lions. Rain had fallen heavily the previous evening, and, judging from the appearance of their spoor, the troop must have passed shortly after it. Big lions and lionesses and young lions had passed along here—fully a dozen I should think—for their spoor left a broad, distinct track in the jungle, along which one might have galloped to follow them up, had it not been for the ever increasing thickness of the bushes. We followed the trail for some distance, but it led deeper and deeper into the forest, and the knowledge that the lions must have had such a start of us, and had, perhaps, put a score or two of miles between us since they had passed along here, considerably damped my ardour, and I at length gave it up, and made back for the plain. But that track of their great paws remains very clearly in my mind even now, and I like to imagine to myself the grand picture the moon that night must have looked down upon, as that formidable band went trooping through the gloom of the jungle, now and again sending their great voices out through the night air.

So thick was the bush here that Jama and I lost the rest of the party for some little while, but repeated shots in the air eventually brought us together again outside the jungle. We then spread out in a long line over the great bān, circling towards the little conical hill by which I had shot the lioness and three young lions a few days before. We searched the few clumps of bushes that grew on its bare sides, and drew a blank, and then took a bee-line across the plain for camp. The Somali is a convivial soul, and likes company, and those with me had had more than enough of scouting across country in isolated couples on the look-out for lion. They all drifted together somehow, and rode along a cheery group, much to my dissatisfaction. Suddenly a young oryx sprang away out of the grass from almost under their horses' hoofs. Away went my whole following—Jama excepted —pell-mell after it, spears waving, tobes flying, shouting, and whooping. Soon they were streaming away in the distance over the plain, with one or two of the fastest ponies keeping up well with the oryx. I blessed them and rode on to camp with Jama, which was about eight miles off. Looking back again I saw their distant figures, dismounted, standing round something. The oryx had evidently been speared. I went on and got back to camp by a rather roundabout way. It must have been then nearly 5 o'clock. Just as I had sat down inside my tent, and was reflecting that I was pretty well done up, there was the gallop of a horse outside, and the next moment my servant rushed in to say that Azkar had brought news of four lions. My poor pony had scarcely been relieved of his saddle than it was clapped on again, and, accompanied by Mahomed Ādan, a very smart Somali of mine, I was riding fast back with Azkar in the direction whence we had come. The sky behind was black with thunderclouds, which were fast overtaking us, and, in front of us, the sun low down in the heavens did not promise more than a couple of hours of daylight.

So, there was no sparing the poor ponies, though they were dead tired. What a ride that was! I shall never forget it. It was flog and spur all the way, and that was a good eight miles back again. As we rode, I gathered from Azkar that just as they had cut up and tied the meat of the oryx to their saddles and were riding off, several lions had come trotting through the grass towards the spot, attracted by the hovering vultures overhead. I then remembered how often Somalis have urged me to remain concealed near the carcase of some game I had shot, on the chance of lion or leopard being drawn to the spot by the sight of the gathering vultures in the sky, but had pooh-poohed it as a fanciful idea of theirs; but here were their words come true enough, and it is reasonable to conclude that lions are wont to watch to sky at times for such signs. Azkar had ridden hard back to me at once, leaving the other four to mark the lions, of whom he thought there were four, but was not certain. By the time we had cleared the jungle, and reached the plain, the ponies had scarcely a canter left in them, and we were all equally exhausted with urging the poor beasts on. To add to our difficulties the black sky overhead opened on to us a veritable deluge. Down came the rain with a hiss, refreshing us with wet skins, but rendering the ground so slippery that our ponies' legs were sliding all ways, and we had to hold them up as well as send them along. The rain, however, did not last long, but overhead, and all along the mountains to the left, the sky remained very threatening, though the western horizon before us still showed clear and bright, with the sun unpleasantly low in it. We had some distance yet to ride over the slopes of the plain, and it took a good half-hour more of flogging and spurring, by which time there was not the ghost of a canter left in our animals, before we came in sight of the horsemen on the plain. They were scattered, riding here and there, some towards us, evidently following something in the grass, which something, as I drew nearer, I made out to be a lion. In one direction a big yellow beast is bounding easily away in front of one of the horsemen, to which Mahomed Ādan points out shouting, "Libah! libah!" (lion). But they are nearer than that, for the next moment my eyes fall on two more large, yellow animals, walking calmly along through the grass, one behind the other, followed by a Somali at a respectful distance.

Azkar and his pony are completely done up, but Ādan and I are just able to hustle our animals into a shambling run, and ride up to within seventy yards of the pair of lionesses, for such they turn out to be. I jumped to the ground, handing my pony to Ādan, and hurriedly crammed my pockets full of cartridges from the bag he carried. The nearer Somalis are wild with excitement, and are shouting out something to us. "What is it they say, Ādan?" "Five lions, sahib." Heavens, what a dream of bliss! I was in a hurry to realize it, and ran after the pair. The hindmost lioness was a big, gaunt, old-looking animal, with a very nonchalant air about her, as she walks calmly along, as if indisposed to be disturbed by any one. In front of her was another full-grown lioness, with a glossy, yellow skin, but with a less imperturable air. I aimed at the old lioness, but my hand shook so from the hard ride, that I could not keep on her, and, vainly endeavouring to get steady, I fired and missed. She took not the slightest notice of the report of the rifle. Again I fired—again a miss. She turned her head this time, and looked at me, but stalked on as casually as before. This was pretty shooting, indeed, and five lions to bag! I felt desperate, and ran towards her, within twenty yards or so, and fired into her left side, behind the shoulder. She sprang into the air, turned completely over, then down she came, and lay quite still. There was no time to look at her. I passed her by, and ran after the other lioness, who had begun to run at the firing. As I ran, shouts from the Somalis attracted my attention. "Nar māro, sahib!" (shoot the male) called Mahomed Ādan, who was riding near. Suddenly, to my left, I saw a dark, grim head above the grass observing me. It was a lioness—though at the time we all took it for a maneless lion from its great size—crouching not twenty paces from me, and I was running past it. As soon as I stopped and turned towards her, she greeted me with snarls, open jaws, and a flicking of the tail, which brought me to my knee at once, and I fired into her chest. At the shot she gave a great leap backwards, and disappeared in the grass. The next few moments were exciting, for I supposed I had a wounded lion to deal with, and there being no time for caution, I had to follow up quickly.

But I was relieved to find her lying stretched out, quite still, on her side. She seemed dead enough, but I could not stop to see, and hastened off after the companion of the one I had first shot. I soon came close upon her, crouched in the grass, with her head down. She also received me with a growl, and her tail flicked the ground. I replied at once, hitting her in the centre of the nose, though I had aimed for below her chin. She dropped her head to the shot, and never moved again.

I hailed Mahomed Ādan, who had stuck close to me like a brick, to bring up my pony, and in another instant was in the saddle again, spurring hard in the direction, where I saw another yellow beauty, some four hundred yards away, bounding gaily over the plain, with one of the horsemen urging his tired beast slowly in her wake. I cut in to intercept her from the far distant line of jungle, for which she was making; but she continued her way at an easy canter, and all I could do was to ride alongside at a little distance off her, hoping that my company would annoy her into coming to bay, whilst I had leisure to admire her splendid power and shape as she bounded over the grass. Suddenly she stopped, swung round and looked at me. I pulled up too, then the next moment she was charging straight for me. At the time I thought I was caught, remembering my pony was dead beat, but I suppose the latter saw its danger too, for, with equal suddenness, we turned tail, and were making a flying retreat before the lioness. She did not pursue us very far, and again laid down in the grass. I pulled up some forty yards away from her, and waited until one of the Somalis, who was riding towards me, came up. I then dismounted and proceeded to load, and I very well recollect the next few moments were rather uncomfortable, for as I searched hurriedly in my pockets for solid-bullet cartridges, and, of course, hollow ones, with the usual perversity of things, would only turn up, the lioness lay in the grass, making it unpleasant for me with a continuous angry growling, which sounded very much as if she was coming on at any moment. At last I was loaded with the right kind, and having walked forward a little way, sat down and fired at her chest. At the shot, a very shaky one, which only slightly wounded her inside the forearm, she sprang up and charged straight for me. I jumped to my feet and aimed at her chest, but, good heavens! how my arm shook. The exhausting ride back, and the subsequent running, had set every nerve and muscle "on the jump." To and fro swayed the muzzles of my rifle, now on her, now very much off her, and for the life of me I could not steady myself. My second gun was nowhere, and my right barrel empty. It looked bad for me, I thought, and I must hang on to my only shot until she was almost on me. How long that wait of a second or two seemed, while the lioness charged over the forty paces of level ground between us, I very well remember, and more than once my finger pressed more heavily on the trigger, but I held on, fortunately for me I believe. On and on she comes, and still I see my aim wavers. Now she is within eight or ten paces of me, and in another instant I must fire, when, great is my surprise and intense my relief, she stops dead right before me, and glances to her left. I look at her one moment in astonishment, see her right shoulder exposed, change my aim on it instantly and fire, and the thinning smoke reveals her stretched out on her side a few paces from me. What caused her to stop almost at the end of her charge? Either her heart failed her, or, more probably I think, because she heard the gallop of an approaching horseman, who was riding up to see the fun. For when she stopped, her head was turned in that direction. "Where's the fifth?" I ask, but the reply is, "Māfish" (no more), and even Azkar seems to think I have had enough, remarking that he thought the last had got me, and that he was prepared to come to my assistance. Well, I thought I must give up the fifth, there being no time to search, for the sun was very near setting behind the peaks, casting a glow of pink and gold over the western sky.

Indeed, there did not seem time enough to skin the four we had got; so, leaving one man to mark the spot where the last one lay, I rode off with Azkar and another Somali to look up the others, scanning the ground on all sides for a sight of the fifth, for I was loth to let it escape. Suddenly Azkar cried out, "Wākā" (there it is), and there I saw, in the direction he pointed, the very animal, a lioness, seemingly some hundred yards off, bounding away through the grass. We gave chase as fast as our tired ponies could go, and after a little while drew near her. Hearing us overtaking her, she stopped and crouched in the grass, and we pulled up too. I commenced operations by dismounting and sitting on the grass to rest, and steady myself a bit too, for I was about dead beat, and, after my experience with No. 4, I entered with much less confidence than usual into the encounter with No. 5. But the light over the plain was growing too dim to allow of more than a few moments, and then I got up and walked towards her, whereupon she commenced to snarl and growl at me. At about thirty yards from her I sat down to fire, for it was the only position I could hope to get a steady aim, but the light was so bad, and the waving grass got into my line of sight, that I dropped my rifle again, and went on nearer, devoutly hoping that she would be content with snarling. I wanted no more charges that day. When somewhat nearer, I again sat down, got my aim on the point of her shoulder and pressed the trigger. As my rifle rang out—simultaneously seemingly—she gave a great spring into the air, her back curved like a bow. I let drive the left barrel into her whilst in the air, making a rather pretty shot, for it hit her fairly behind the shoulder, and down she came to the ground in a lump, dying. Going up to her, I noticed, as I had in the case of several others, that she had seized a forearm in her jaws, into which she was biting convulsively. I was glad as I watched that it was no portion of myself. Soon the lioness lay still enough, and so, while the sun was setting, within half an hour, I had bagged five full-grown lionesses. To me a most memorable sunset. Very jubilant were we all at the huge stroke of luck, as we shook hands all round. But the fast disappearing daylight cut short our rejoicings, and I felt anxious for my skins, for it seemed impossible to get them off before dark fell. But it was done, and well done, by Mahomed Ādan and another Somali alone. The former worked like a Trojan, doing the giant's share. I give it as an instance of what real good stuff there is in Somalis. Indian sportsmen, who have experienced the want of steam power in the ordinary native, can appreciate their performance.

A HALF-HOUR'S BAG. [*p.* 96.

It was a wild scene I looked upon, as I sat resting beside a dead lioness, waiting for them to be done. The day was dying fast. Pale lights lingered low in the heavens behind the solitary peaks, where the sun had gone down. From the mountains, reaching over our heads, rain-clouds spread like a black pall in the sky. A cold, white mist crept over the ground, shrouding the scattered figures of men and horses. Altogether, very drear and inhospitable looked the great plain in the waning light, and the spirits sank chilled before its vast solitude.

At length we gather together in the darkness, laden with the skins, heavy with the heads and paws intact in them, to where the hobbled ponies are grazing. Tying them on to the terrified ponies takes some time, and then we move slowly across the plain, seeking, or rather feeling, for the track which will lead towards camp. After a while the feel of the ground under our horses' hoofs told us we had struck it. Our pace is a walk, for the tired-out animals can do no more. And the riders are not much better, for none of us have had a scrap of food since early morning. As for myself, I had a mouth as dry as a limekiln from a raging thirst, but soon the rain came down in sheets and bucketfuls from the black sky overhead and rid me of it. I lay on my face on the ground and drank delicious cold draughts of the rain-water as it ran in streams down the track.

Then we continued at a wearisome walk for another couple of hours, our animals slipping and sliding, while the rain continued to drench us to the skin. But sitting, fagged out, stiff, and cold, in the drenching rain as we were, those five skins to me, and, of course, the promised bakshish to my men, made very light of it all. At length, as we rode out of the plain into a belt of tall mimosa tree-jungle, the rain ceased, and soon, right before us, above the dark trees, from out a misty bank of clouds, a full moon rose, wondrously pure and bright, as if bathed in the heavy night's rain, and bright stars began to peep out through rents in the black heavens.

It was a beautiful scene, and my irrepressible Somalis, unconsciously perhaps, showed their appreciation of it by breaking out into song, and, as we passed, several karias aroused their sleeping inhabitants with wild shouts of the

"Sirkal's great shoot!" At last, about an hour or so before midnight, the black thorn-fence and white tent of our encampment showed up in the moonlight. We galloped up with a flourish, arousing the sleepers. The story of the big shoot is received with much exclamation and rejoicing, for lions slain always meant fat-tailed sheep for their dinners on the morrow. Then dry clothes and an immense dinner of oryx meat set me to rights, and as I lie back in my chair, snug inside my closed tent, cleaning my rifle, within hearing of the cheery voices of the Somalis chatting round a fire outside, I shoot all five lionesses over again, feeling about as jolly as it is possible for mortal to be, and envying no man.

## CHAPTER VII.

THE next day was one long rest spent in photographing heads, pegging out skins, examining bullet-holes, and generally having a delightfully lazy loaf about camp, so pleasant after a successful hard day. The following are the measurements of the five pegged-out skins, which were stretched as little as possible. I give them in the order they were shot :—8 feet 9 inches, 8 feet $11\frac{3}{4}$ inches, 9 feet 2 inches, 8 feet $5\frac{1}{2}$ inches, 8 feet 11 inches. The pure-lead solid bullet which struck the third lioness on the nose was found under the skin beyond the left ribs.

On the following day I went out into the thick jungle near camp for a little shoot after oryx. After having done a couple of unsuccessful and exceedingly painful stalks on my stomach, I was becoming somewhat ruffled as to my feelings, when we espied a solitary oryx standing in a very open piece of ground. It looked no easy matter to get near him. A long line of grazing camels were being driven slowly towards him by a few Somali herdsmen, which, still far enough not to alarm him, we noticed attracted his attention from time to time. So, seizing these unguarded moments, Jama and I worked our way by sudden rushes towards him, collapsing on our faces at full length behind some small bush in time to escape his notice. At last no more cover—beyond the bare, shortish grass—lay between us and the oryx, but it was a long shot, and I did not fancy it, for he was completely head on to us. What was best to be done I wondered, as I lay face down, very short of breath, behind our small cover. I saw, some little distance away to one side of us, a very small bush, which, I thought, if I could gain, might give me a more oblique view on to his flank. I asked Jama what he thought, but his opinion was that I should be seen, and he advised waiting. But the line of camels was drawing closer, and I doubted that the oryx would stand their approach much longer without bolting, for he already looked fidgety, so I made up my mind to try for the small bush, and commenced a crawl on my stomach through the grass that would have made a snake envious. I reached the bush at last undetected, and breathless, but in very little better position for a shot than before. The bush was so small, too, that the least movement in attempting to sit up and fire would be pretty sure to be detected, and as I was lying I would have to fire through the bush, which was awkward. While I lay thinking it over, the oryx helped me out of the situation by starting round, and staring at my little shelter, exposing his left flank to me in doing so. I was evidently discovered, and he would be off in another instant. I sprang to one side of the bush exposing myself to the astounded gaze of the oryx, and fired at his shoulder before he had sufficiently recovered to bolt. It was really rather a pretty shot at about two hundred yards. He dropped to it at once, and lay on his back kicking. We ran up, and, with the help of the herdsmen, who, not having seen us, were much astonished to see the oryx fall so suddenly, and equally delighted with new-born hopes of coming in for some of the flesh, we performed the necessary halal to make good Mahommedan meat of him. My satisfaction at getting the beast was the more jubilant on finding that I had bagged a really good head. The length of the horns was good, but not remarkable, but their thickness was unusual. I wish I had the measurement by me to give.

That night a lion raided a karia very close to my camp, carrying off a sheep. We tried to follow on his spoor the next morning, but failed. My good friend Azkar now left me for a time, having received news that his karia had had a fight with another, and that there were killed and wounded on both sides. This is an every-day occurrence almost to the fight-loving Somali; still, as dead men meant blood-money, it was only a matter of business to go and see to it. So Azkar went off nominally to restore the peace, and, at his request, I let him have two of my rifle-men as an escort, as well as, by the dignity of their weapons as servants of the "Sirkal," to impose the *pax Britannica* on the belligerents, he having promised faithfully not to enlist their support to drub the enemy.

Raiding the camel and cattle of another tribe is an amusement to which the Somal is very partial. A party of horsemen will make a dash into the territory of a neighbouring tribe, descend upon the often unprotected herds of camels, etc., grazing in the jungle, and drive them off before them, not omitting, so they have told me in conversation, to put to the spear the few unfortunate herdsmen in charge of the animals, even though they may be boys and women. Indeed, whilst I was in my present camp a party of horsemen rode off, so I was told, with the intention of doing a similar friendly act to a neighbouring tribe of the Ogaden, about a day's march from us. And I well remember one afternoon, when reading inside my tent, I heard a noise of shouting and horses galloping past my zareba. On running out to inquire, I saw a score of horsemen galloping away with wild shouts and a flourish of spears. My own people were much excited also, and told me that some of the Ogaden had raided the camels of the karias near me—which I thought highly interesting, and quite in accord with the wild surroundings; but when they added that all my camels were probably grazing in company with those of the karias, I saw the whole thing in altogether a different light, and felt as bloodthirsty as any

Somali. Fortunately it turned out to be nothing more than a scare, and the returning horsemen drew up outside my zareba, and went through a kind of war-show in my honour, which consisted in charging about at full tilt, uttering wild cries, and stabbing the air with their spears, just to show, no doubt, what they would have done for the Ogaden, though they merely ended in riding over and nearly killing an aged Somali who got in the way.

Another time a small kāfila, consisting of a few men and women, sought, with lugubrious faces, the protection of my zareba. Their tale was that they had been attacked by some men of one of the big karias near me as they were travelling through the neighbourhood, had had some of their goods taken, and one of their men wounded. The man was produced; he lay like a log on the ground, with a bad spear-wound in his neck. To oblige Azkar, who knew the people, I undertook to interfere, and sent off a couple of my men with rifles, to summon the headmen of the karia, with the culprits, to my zareba. After a little delay, and a second summons, they arrived, and an amicable agreement was come to: the wounded man being compensated with two fat-tailed sheep for the hole in his neck. I give this as a slight instance of the weight the English name now carries throughout a great extent of Somali-land, where, not many years ago, it was not considered safe to travel without a strong escort.

The rainfall was becoming so rare that it would be soon impossible to remain where I was, and I had now to pay attention to the storing of water for our use on the march to the nearest water-holes, some eighty miles distant, if, as I expected, I should have to shortly commence my return march to the coast, unless a messenger, long overdue, arrived very soon with news of an extension of my leave. Washing, accordingly, became a greater luxury than ever, and the heavens were daily scanned for the welcome signs of rain-clouds. But now the sun began to set in cloudless skies, whereas formerly dark banks of clouds had been wont to gather on the horizon at the close of day.

As the water-supply became scarce the Somalis, naturally enough, were reluctant to accompany me, or to hire their ponies out, for the long rides over the country that we had been making. So, one morning, a couple of days after I had bagged the oryx with the good head, I rode out, accompanied only by two horsemen and Jama, to search for lion. We took the usual direction, down into the grassy bān, keeping a short distance from the broad tract of jungle which fringed the base of the mountains. I was riding alone, the others scattered out singly to my right, some three or four hundred yards apart. As I walked my horse through the long, dry grass, my eyes almost mechanically sweeping the ground in my front for sight or signs of the royal game, I watched indifferently an oryx galloping off across me, and then, as my eyes again passed over the ground, I noticed an animal of a brownish yellow moving through the grass some distance ahead of me, but scarcely gave it a thought, taking it for some oryx or gazelle. However, as I rode on, the animal again caught my eye, and the thought occurred to me that it was rather a queer shape for an oryx, and its walk, though familiar, was a most un-oryx like one. "Where are its horns?" and, "Surely it can't be a lion," were my next almost simultaneous thoughts, as I rammed my heels into the pony's flanks and rode fast towards it.

As I drew nearer, great was my joy, for I could distinguish the outlines and walk of a lion. Good heavens, what luck again! I shouted and waved my rifle to attract the notice of the Somalis, and galloped hard towards the animal. I soon came alongside of a heavy-looking brute, which my approach caused to break into a trot, and then into a slow canter. I rode alongside for some little time, admiring its massive proportions and the powerful swing of its stride through the grass.

The lioness, for it turned out to be one, though from her great size I had at first taken her for a maneless lion, had evidently been making a mighty meal quite recently; for her stomach reached low to the ground, and her slow, heavy bounds over the ground did not promise to continue far. But I was in no hurry to shoot, for the line of jungle towards which she was making was at a comfortable distance off, and it was intense pleasure to me to watch the splendid brute moving over the ground—a perfect picture of strength—as I rode along in her company, at a respectful distance. But, as I had expected from the size of her stomach, she soon found the pace inconvenient, and suddenly stopped, faced round, and crouched on the ground, observing me. One of the Somalis only had arrived on the scene as I dismounted, and tied my animal to a small thorn-bush close by. She gave me a growl or two while I did so, and now lay, with her head held low, watching me as I walked towards her.

A lion's yellow eyes, as I had now more than once experienced, are singularly impressive if you happen to be watching them some thirty paces off with merely the bare, level ground between you, while you observe their regard is fixed on you. They incline one to caution, and it was with much of that in my movements that I partially circled round her in order to get a shot at the shoulder, followed by her eyes as I did so, watching on my part intently for the first sign of a coming charge. But she merely growled at me, and when I got the required position I took a standing shot at the point of her left shoulder. She sprang into the air, convulsively curled up. Immediately she touched the ground again, I fired the left barrel into her chest, upon which she dropped her head, seized her left forearm in her jaws, and lay motionless for some time. But she soon came to, and struggled to get up, looking very savagely at me, making me step back in a hurry, for I had gone up close thinking she was done for, and was standing gazing admiringly at her. My first bullet had struck the shoulder, and the second had pierced the chest, which ought to have been sufficient, but as she continued her efforts to struggle on to her feet I gave her another bullet behind the shoulder, upon which she raised her head opened her great jaws wide, then rolled over on to her side, and died. Though her skull is not the largest of the lionesses that I had shot, she looked of more massive proportions than any of them, and was indeed a superbly powerful brute. On opening her stomach we found she was gorged with oryx flesh. She had evidently killed one out on the plain during the night, and, having made her huge meal off it, was returning to the shelter of the jungle somewhat late in the morning when I came across her. Unfortunately, I did not measure any of my lions in the customary way, viz. along the curves, so it is useless to give here the measurements I took for comparison. Her pegged-out skin measures 9 feet 1 inch.

Leaving Jama to remove the skin, I rode on with the other two Somalis, and came on to fresh spoor of another lioness, which had crossed the plain into the jungle that morning. We tracked them up very slowly, and with great difficulty, until the trail led us into the broad tract of jungle where the earth, being less closely covered with grass, the tracking became easier and more rapid. Following on the spoor of an animal is to my mind the most interesting form of hunting on foot, but, when it happens to be a lion, the keenness of the sport is intense. The long follow-up, with all its alternating hopes and fears, now so slow and difficult, then faster, now in the depths of despair over the trail lost, then once more jubilant in a lucky cast, and when at last the ground betrays the great brute's recent presence with fresher signs, how hot the excitement grows, until the sudden sight of the lion himself thrills through you with an eager delight. And so it was with me that day. We followed faster and more surely on her tracks as they became fresher and clearer, telling us she was no great distance ahead. Hot and intense was the sense of expectation as one's eyes searched the bushes ahead for the first glimpse of her.

At last we come to a place where it is apparent she has been lying quite recently, and, when we find ground freshly damp from her urine, huge is my joy and fiery my impatience to sight her, and I begin to include her in my total of lions. But, alas! for the proverbial slip. I was dismounted, following closely behind the tracker, with rifle cocked, eyeing the surrounding bushes keenly, when suddenly I view the lioness sitting under a bush some fifty yards ahead. At that very instant the other Somali, who is behind us with the ponies, shouts out, " Wā kā " (there it is). Before I can throw up my rifle to fire, something yellow flashed through the bushes, and the lioness was gone! We chased her on horseback through the thick jungle, which grew rapidly denser, but though we sighted her once or twice, she gave us the slip again, and we eventually lost all traces of her. As neither of my companions could understand one word I said, I had not even the satisfaction of impressing on the man who had called out, what an idiot he was, so had to consume my own wrath as I rode back to camp.

## CHAPTER VIII.

THERE being still no signs of the long-expected messenger from the coast, bearing news of more leave for me, I could not delay my return march any longer. Therefore, the next morning I rode out, in company with some of my Somali friends, to take a regretful farewell of the wild bit of country I had, with good reason, grown fond of. In the fresh air of the early morning we rode briskly down the grassy, bush-covered slopes leading to the plain, and scouted over its breezy levels over much the same ground that we had ridden the previous day. As we inclined towards the fringe of open bush and long grass jungle which marked the line where forest and plain met, soon signals from Jama brought us at a gallop to where he stood gazing at the ground. And very full of significance was that particular patch of ground at which he stared, for its grass was crushed and stained with blood, and lions' spoor were written in its soil. It told its tale clearly enough. Lions had pulled down and devoured some animal here during the night, and, from the scanty remnants of skin and a hoof or two found in searching the spot, it appeared that the unlucky beast had been a Soemmering's gazelle.

We followed up the spoor with much difficulty, as the ground was plentifully covered with short grass hereabouts, and after making very little progress the Somalis lost the trail altogether. We were reluctantly about to abandon the pursuit, when one of the horsemen, who had penetrated a little way into the bush, came riding back to say that he had struck the fresh spoor of a lion a short distance ahead of us. This made us cheerful again. We followed him to the spot, and started on the track, which proved much easier to take up, as it led over more bare soil between clumps of bushes. By the size of the spoor, they were evidently those of a male lion, which from their appearance the Somalis judged to have passed along here in the early hours of the morning. He was very probably one of the murderous gang who had devoured the gazelle. Surely, though often very slowly, we followed on his lordly footsteps, often at a standstill, and obliged to cast about, for many a time there was but the ghost of an impression of his paws on the dry earth. Sometimes the trail seemed lost, but a lucky cast ahead would save us from despair, revealing the great paws clearly imprinted along the sandy bottom of some shallow rain channel. And so we tracked on for the best part of an hour, the spoor leading us straight into the jungle, where the widely-growing bushes gave place to a denser jungle of small mimosa trees and thickets of bush.

I was riding behind the leading tracker, judging it advisable, from my last experience with the lioness, to be ready to give chase at once if necessary, while the Somalis were dismounted assisting each other to carry on the spoor, when suddenly I saw a yellow animal spring like a flash from one thicket to another, some fifty yards to one side of us, and then disappear. For the moment I took it to be a gazelle, but seeing the Somalis crouched forward staring in that direction, I looked again—when lo! a heavy-looking lion and lioness trotted away from out the same thicket. I put spurs to my pony and dashed off after them. But the jungle was far too close to allow of such a pace. Thorny mimosa trees caught us with their branches, thorny bush got in our way and severely mauled us, and, to add to my discomfiture, a branch knocked my "shikar topee" over my eyes, blinding me most effectually for a few moments, while, rifle in one hand and reins in the other, I was powerless to rid myself of it, nor able to guide my pony as he careered at full gallop through the thorn-trees. However, I managed to shake it off at length, and my good little pony had carried me so staunchly through the thorny jungle that I soon came up with the lion, who looked a great deal too heavy to be good at running, nor did he appear to be exerting himself to do so. He was a hugely massive animal, but had only a very small, yellow mane. The lioness, as I came up, darted to one side, leaving us together. He trotted on a few more yards, then turned suddenly aside, and crouched in some grass by a clump of bushes facing towards me.

I pulled up and halloed for some one to hold

my pony. A Somali soon joined me and caught my reins, while I reconnoitred towards the lion, to choose my shot as he lay growling at us some twenty paces off. Getting a clear view at his shoulder, I fired at it. He appeared to be badly hit, but as he continued to growl loudly, I let him have the left barrel in the same place, upon which his head dropped. Jama just then rode up, carrying my topee on the end of his spear, having amused himself by tent-pegging at it as he followed me. He said the lioness was also marked down; so, thinking the lion done for, I hurried off after his mate. I found her at bay not very far off, watched by a Somali. She had taken her stand behind a perfect screen of green, formed by two small trees and a bush growing close together, the whole draped with a mass of creeper, through which I could see her yellow face watching me as I walked towards her from the other side. But as I hesitated to fire at her head, something caused her to turn and look behind her. It must have been one of the Somalis who, in searching for me, was unconsciously riding down on her rear. This was a diversion in my favour, for it gave me a glimpse of her right shoulder, and I fired through the screen at it  I was so close to her, only fifteen paces off, as I afterwards measured, that it was impossible to miss the spot aimed at. She rolled over, or rather vanished from view. Running round the screen, over a red earth anthill covered with grass, I found her lying on her side practically dead. My shot had struck behind the right shoulder, and passed clean through and out on the other side. There was now the other lioness to be thought of—for it was a lioness, and no gazelle, that I had seen to spring between the bushes. Greatly was I chagrined to find that one of the Somalis, after having ridden her down, had left her to see what I was doing. Jama and the smart Somali who had followed up the lioness I had just shot at once started with me to track her. The spoor led deep into the jungle, where riding out of a walk would be exceedingly difficult. I had gone on a little ahead of the trackers, to take a look round, when I suddenly viewed the lioness trotting away in front of me. I rode in pursuit, shouting to warn the others, but soon lost her in the dense bush. Having searched in vain for traces of her, we gave her up, and were riding back when suddenly one of the men espied her inside a very thick bush. She had evidently crouched, and I had ridden past her, thinking she was on ahead. I jumped to the ground, and walked a little way round the bush, in order to pick my shot, when, to my utter disgust, she slipped out on the farther side and disappeared—and for good this time. Having given up further search for her as hopeless, we rode back to where I had shot the lion, and I was very sorry to find the poor old fellow still alive. He had managed to drag himself into some long grass a few yards off, where I heard him growl as I approached. I could not get a clear shot at his heart, and had to put two more bullets into his shoulder before he died. The lion, I thought, looked very grand as he lay there helpless to attack, for his shoulder was completely smashed, making one feel somehow at the time more regret at having to kill the noble-looking brute than appreciation of one's luck. And here, with the huge dead lion stretched out on the grass before me, while on the surrounding trees numbers of vultures are already swooping down to sit and bide their time,

AFTER A FAREWELL DAY WITH THE LIONS. [*p.* 120.

here I may well bring these recollections to a close, for the next day saw me in full march back to the coast, regretting each step that led away from those vast grassy bāns, dark mimosa jungles, and picturesque wadis of that wild and fascinating land, which is ever calling to drink of its waters once more.

# PIGSTICKING
## IN THE SOMALI COUNTRY, EAST AFRICA.

When quartered at Aden, in 1887, I was sent across the Gulf on detachment duty to a place called Zaila, in the Somali country, on the east coast of Africa. Before leaving Aden I had heard from a friend, who had done some shooting in that country, of the number of pig to be seen there, and the great possibilities that the country offered for first-rate pigsticking. So interesting, indeed, were the descriptions that I received of the African boar, or wart hog, of its enormous tushes and extraordinary and formidable appearance, that my keenness to make its acquaintance became quite uncomfortable, and I felt I should never know peace of mind again until I had tried my hand at spearing him. So not many days passed by after my arrival at Zaila before

I started off for a week's pigsticking to a place called Uhdhawadiri, some twenty-five miles distant, where the Somalis told me there were plenty of "dofār" (pig). I left Zaila early in the afternoon, my following consisting of two of my sepoys, a syce and servant, and two Somalis of the Eesa tribe, the one as a camel-driver, and the other as my shikari—the latter named Abdullah. It was my intention to encamp for the night at Warabōd, a halting place about ten miles distant, which we reached towards sunset. Warabōd (meaning in Somali the place of hyænas) was merely a dry, sandy river-bed, or, perhaps, I should rather call it torrent bed, where water could be obtained by digging a hole a few feet deep in the dried-up, sandy bottom of the torrent course. Here and there wells had been made by the nomad Somalis for watering their droves of camels, and it was to these wells, Abdullah assured, me that the pig in the neighbourhood would come to drink at sunrise and sunset. The wadi ran through a very open plain, stretching to the horizon, thinly covered with a dry grass, and dotted with clumps of bushes. Better going could not have been wished for. In one direction, only about a mile and a half from the wells, there stretched a long, dark line of jungle, which was not practicable for riding, as I was very shortly to find out.

While my followers were pitching my tent under a tree some little distance from the water, I took my gun, and set off to stalk a bustard, which I espied enjoying a quiet evening stroll in the neighbourhood. Having got near the bird, I was about to take a pot shot at him when, from the direction of my camp, mingled cries in Hindustani and Somali of "Dukkah!" "Dofār!" (pig) greeted my ears. Truly, never before had native voices sounded so pleasantly. Entirely ignoring the bustard, I rushed off towards my camp, where my syce was hurriedly saddling my horse, and there, not more than one hundred yards away, stood a couple of splendid African wart hog, who had no doubt come for their evening drink, but were scared off at seeing my people. Quite prepared as I had been to behold an animal differing somewhat remarkably from the ordinary boar, I was completely astonished by the extraordinary appearance of the brutes in front of me. They stood still and gazed at us for some seconds, and I, too, by way of returning the compliment, took stock of them, whilst the syce was giving the last touches to my horse's girths. My eye was first caught by the great size of their heads and by the gleam of their enormous white tushes, which stood out grandly on each side of their broad snouts, and showed up well against the dark grey of their bodies. Along their backs lay a mane of long, reddish-brown bristles, which seemed to stand half erect as they boldly stared at us. They certainly were grand-looking brutes, and their formidable appearance had not been exaggerated. The large, fleshy protuberances beneath the eye and near the snout, which give this animal its name of wart hog, and add an almost diabolical look to its ferocious appearance, I was at the time too far off to see distinctly; and, as I was destined to have a very much closer inspection of the animal later on, I will not now anticipate by any further description. No doubt, having decided in their piggish minds that we were a nuisance, and that there was to be no drink for them that evening, they turned round, and calmly trotted off. In another moment

I was in the saddle, and was galloping after them. Hearing the thud of my horse's hoofs, the boars, to my great surprise, stopped and turned round, as if quite unable to understand what could be following them. Apparently, however, deciding very quickly that we meant business that boded them no good, they dashed off together towards the jungle at a long, bounding gallop. More sporting-looking beasts cannot be imagined, as they sailed away over the plain, their long tuft-ended tails held gaily in the air, and manes flying in the wind. Away they bounded, scarce more than a hundred yards ahead. It was a glorious sight, and made the blood fairly leap in my veins as I rode.

My horse, an Arab, and a veteran pigsticker, had evidently recognized the genus of the two beauties in front of us, and, with ears pricked forward and flying tail, was pulling like a fiend to get away. "Go along, old boy!" I cried, as I gave him his head, and my good nag now tore over the ground in hot pursuit. The jungle was unpleasantly close, and I saw that I must ride hard, and make the running as hot as possible, if I meant to get in a spear at all.

The boars were keeping well together, and as I rode I remember how full of anxiety I was as to which owned the largest tushes, at the same time regretting sorely that I could not bag them both. My horse was going splendidly; half a mile was soon covered, and yet I seemed to have gained nothing on the boars. "Surely this pace can never last," thought I, as I looked anxiously at the now rapidly-nearing jungle, and urged on my horse the harder. Another quarter mile was cleared before the pace began to tell decidedly. The boars had separated, and I had now singled out the possessor of the largest tushes. Nearer and nearer I crept up, and, when within twenty yards or so, in went the spurs, and with a rush my horse carried me alongside the flying boar. I speared him as he jinked sharply off at right angles. With the very best intentions, I had levelled the spear for behind his shoulder; but the jink had saved him, my spear merely entering his hind quarters. However, I could claim first blood. The touch of cold steel only served to rouse the boar's pluck, for I had scarcely got my horse round when I found him, to my great delight, charging straight for us. I quickly decided not to allow the owner of such a pair of tushes to catch my horse at a standstill, and so, spurring, I rode to meet the charging brute. My plucky horse carried me straight at him, without swerving an inch; but my spear, striking the boar's forehead, was thrown up, and the boar, with a vicious grunt, charged in under the horse, ripping up at his flank as he ran in. Fortunately, however, his tushes caught against my riding-boot, and my horse got clear of him without a scratch. The boar then made for the jungle, the edge of which he gained by the time I caught him up. At first, the jungle being thin, I was able to follow him with some little difficulty; but whenever I endeavoured to spear, he promptly dodged me behind the bushes. Several attempts to spear in this way only resulted in my riding into trunks of trees or thick bushes. The jungle now became quite close, and I began to fear that I should lose him. At last, however, he gave me a chance, for, apparently wearied with my pressing intentions, the boar turned round and faced me, as if meditating another charge. I seized my opportunity, and, forgetting tree trunks and bushes, rode at him. This time I succeeded in spearing him well in the right side. As I delivered my spear, I found my horse had carried me into a thick clump of high bushes. If the boar at this moment had only turned his attention to my horse, he might have put a stop to our further pigsticking for some time. Fortunately, he did not do so; but, whilst we were entangled in the thicket, he took his opportunity to decamp. When I at length got clear my friend was nowhere to be seen. I rode about looking for him everywhere, but to no purpose, and felt quite frantic at the thought of losing such a splendid beast.

While continuing my search in a most disconsolate frame of mind, Abdullah came up carrying my second spear. I told him what had happened, and led him back to the place where I had first lost the boar. Abdullah had soon taken up the pugs, and was following them up rapidly, while I, with reviving hopes, followed on foot, leading my horse through the now thick jungle. We had not gone very far when Abdullah showed me some marks of blood on the ground, and against the trunk of a tree, and then, looking about him, he suddenly pointed to a large tree about forty yards off, under which I beheld, to my great joy, the boar sitting upon his hind quarters, and watching us with a very vicious expression on his countenance. The blood was flowing from the last wound I had given him, but there seemed plenty of life in him still. Being afraid to lose him again if I attempted to ride at him in such close ground, I decided to go in on foot, for it was my only chance of getting his tushes. So, throwing the reins to Abdullah, I walked towards the boar, holding my spear at the charge as I advanced, Abdullah the while encouragingly crying out to me, " Khabardār, sahib! khabardār! bara khirab jānwar!" (take care, sahib—a very wicked animal). The boar watched my approach, and, as I drew near him, up he rose, and, giving a savage grunt, charged straight for me. His great head seemed to entirely cover his chest, and I saw that it was practically impossible for me to spear him in front; for, if I should attempt to do so, I felt sure my spear would only strike his head, be knocked up, and he would be in at me. To await his charge until he should almost reach me, and then to spring aside and spear him as he rushed by, was, I thought, my best and almost sole chance; but I half feared that, being in heavy riding-boots, and tired from my hard ride, I should scarcely be quick enough. Long as it may seem in description, there was hardly time, in reality, for thinking or hesitating. In another moment the boar was on me. I took my chance, and stood his charge, as it seemed to me, almost up to the point of my spear, and then, jumping quickly aside, ran the spear well home into his ribs on the left flank. There was a charm and novelty about the situation that one could not fail to appreciate. My great desire to make a close acquaintance with the African wart-hog, was now granted far more fully than I had ever dreamt of, and I gazed with the deepest interest at this formidable-looking beast, now fixed on the other end of my spear—at its great tushes, and the large, unsightly, fleshy protuberances on its hideous face, which struck me at the time as being as absurdly grotesque as it was ferocious and diabolical. There we stood, the boar and I, in this interesting situation, for some moments. He at one end of the spear, eyeing me most

"JUMPING QUICKLY ASIDE, I RAN THE SPEAR WELL HOME INTO HIS RIBS." [*p.* 131.

viciously out of his fierce, wicked little eyes, I at the other, lost in admiration of his big tushes and general appearance, and wondering how I was to win against such an ugly-looking customer. Indeed, I felt by no means confident of coming off best in the encounter. However, the points were in my favour, and I determined to keep them. I was far too tired to run the risk of withdrawing the spear for another thrust, for I felt I could not be quick enough at such close quarters, and so decided to wait and see what the boar meant to do. At first, doubtless exhausted from his hard run and the blood that he had lost from his last wound, he stood quite still, making no struggle to get off the spear-point, and seemed to be meditating on his next move, looking at me in a "tone of voice" as if to say, "Wait till I do get at you." He did not keep me waiting long, and soon commenced a furious attack, at one time pressing furiously against the spear in his efforts to reach me, at another struggling and writhing to get off the spear-head, champing and grinding his tushes, and foaming from the mouth in his rage, whilst I hung on like grim death to the other end of the spear, and endeavoured to bury its head deeper into the boar's side. In this, however, I was by no means successful; the spear-head, having apparently struck against the ribs, refused to penetrate deeper. During the struggle, the shaft of the spear, although a stout bamboo, would bend at times in a highly unpleasant manner, and I began to fear that the possibility of its breaking was not improbable. And so the fight went on for several minutes, till at length, feeling my strength come back to me, I thought it was now my turn to take the initiative, and, during a pause in the boar's struggles, I rapidly withdrew the spear, and, ere the boar could run in at me, had driven it again into his side in a more vital place. It was quite enough —I had won. The gallant old boar, taking his death-wound without a sound, rolled over on his side, and, with another rapid thrust, I put the brave beast out of his pain. A yell of delight from Abdullah greeted my victory. I shall never forget, as I stood over the fallen boar, how pleased I was at having won; and yet I almost felt a feeling of regret for an animal who had shown such a gallant spirit throughout the fight, and had died so pluckily.

The short African twilight was fast changing into a moonless night, as I told Abdullah to run off to the camp and bring my hunting-knife, and also a bottle of beer; and, while he was gone, I sat down by the dead boar, and silently enjoyed my triumph. A calm and perfect sense of enjoyment stole over me as I sat there in the darkening jungle, and recalled the various incidents of the evening's sport. The world somehow seemed to be a pleasant place after all; and I felt a supreme contentment with it, and with all things. Such moments, with all their pleasurable feelings, though perhaps very transitory, still leave us their pleasant memories, to stay with us for many a long day. My horse stood by me, snorting and arching his neck, as he sniffed the dead boar, as if wishing to remind me how well he had served me that day; and I did not forget to acknowledge my plucky old nag's share in the work with an extra large feed on our return to camp.

While waiting here for Abdullah, I may as well take the opportunity to complete my description of the African wart-hog, as I saw him lying before me. I never ceased to regret that I had not brought a measuring-tape with me; for, although I was to be fortunate enough to kill to my own spear a score of boars and sows during my five months' stay at Zaila, this, my first boar, was of larger proportions then any of those I was yet to kill, most of which were apparently full-grown animals. The size of the head, remarkably big in all of them, was, in this boar, quite enormous. From the worn state of his tushes, I should think he must have been rather an old fellow. The tushes of the upper jaw measured (along the outer curve) $8\frac{1}{2}$ inches, and 4 inches, round the thickest part. For the African boar, this measurement is perhaps a little under the average, for many of those that I killed had tushes varying from 9 inches to $9\frac{1}{2}$ inches in length. It is, however, the exceeding massiveness of these upper tushes which makes them appear so enormous, and thus tends to give the wart-hog his formidable aspect. The tushes in the lower jaw measured also $8\frac{1}{2}$ inches, and were very sharp. They are similar to the lower tushes of the Indian boar, but very much straighter. A point which adds to the strange and misshapen appearance of the wart-hog is the almost entire absence of neck, its great head seeming to be literally set on the animal's massive shoulders. The reddish-brown mane of bristles, which I mentioned above, extends along the entire length of the back to the root of the tail. The bristles are quite 2 feet in length (this is the exact measurement of the mane of another boar that I killed). The tail is very long, and is adorned with a tuft of hair at the end.

The Somali wart-hog is rather long in the body, but, from what I saw of them, they do not seem to run to any great height. This one, judging from other full-grown boars that I killed, which were seldom over 30 inches in height, probably stood somewhat over 31 inches. The skin of the animal is of a darkish grey or slate colour.

There was scant time to examine the boar, for darkness had soon come on, and I had been wondering for some while when Abdullah would return, and thinking of how I should enjoy that bottle of beer, when my reflections were at length interrupted by the hullooing of Abdullah, who was trying to find out my whereabouts in the jungle. My answering shout soon brought him and one of my sepoys to where I was sitting.

The latter proceeded to cut off the boar's head (for Abdullah was far too good a Mussulman to touch it), whilst I enjoyed that bottle of Bass with a relish I have never experienced before or since.

When the head was off we started for camp, leaving the remains of the old boar to the jackals, who, uttering their shrill, melancholy howls, had been gathering in the darkness of the bushes close by, eager to devour the evening meal they had already scented.

## CHAPTER II.

THE pale light of dawn was yet hardly visible in the east when my little camp was all astir. My syce had rubbed down my horse, and given him his early morning feed by the time I sallied out of my tent to enjoy the delicious cool of dawn in the tropics, and to partake of the " chota hazaree " ready for me outside my tent. I was soon mounted, and, accompanied by Abdullah, rode out into the grey plain, now fast lightening up under the rays of coming day, in search of the early-rising boar. We roamed about, keeping a middle course between the wells and the line of jungle; for, according to Abdullah, the wart hog would be coming at daybreak to the water, to take their drink to last them through the heat of the day. However, the morning air must have proved too chilly for them on this occasion, for not a single pig of either sex put in an appearance. Strain my eyes

## Pigsticking in the Somali Country. 139

as I might over the wide plain, I could see nothing except now and then a few African gazelle, which I did not not consider worth going after, when there was a chance of meeting wart hog. While thus scanning intently the surrounding plain as I rode along, my fancy would often play me false, picturing the form of a boar in some dark bush, and I would gallop towards it, all eagerness, only to pull up disgusted with my too vivid imagination The sun was high up in the heavens, and had been making itself felt for some time, far more than was agreeable, when I gave up my search, and rode back to camp. We first, however, went into the jungle to visit the spot where I had killed the boar the previous evening. A few gnawed bones, and the ground covered with the pugs of jackal, with here and there the larger pug of the hyæna, told us of the wild orgie the ravenous inhabitants of the jungle had held in the night.

After breakfast and a short rest, I gave orders to break up camp and to start for Uhdhawadiri. The camel, a most cantankerous beast, after having had his head tied down to his legs in a manner painful to behold, and after many a deep objurgation showered on his head from my several followers, at length consented to be loaded, and a start was made. Our course lay over the open plain that stretched before us; there was no track nor landmark that I could notice, and how Abdullah found his way was quite a mystery to me.

And here let me give a description of Abdullah, for whom I took a great liking as he strode along beside my pony, his cheery face a pleasant contrast to the sulky countenances of my Indian followers, who evidently considered their sahib quite " dewanah" (mad) to march in the heat of the day. Abdullah's appearance was novel, if not exactly picturesque. He sported a most wonderful head of hair, reaching down to his shoulders, in small, crinkly locks, and dyed a light red, contrasting somewhat remarkably with his pleasant black countenance.

The features of the Somali are small and rather well made, and, as far as I observed, the only signs of the negro race in them was the hair, which was certainly rather woolly. I asked Abdullah why he grew such a head of hair, and why he did not shave it, or keep it short, like most of his Somali brethren, and Abdullah replied, "Achcha dekna ke wasti, sahib, aurat mangta," which meant that Abdullah wished to look nice and fetch the women, and that he was in want of a wife. Abdullah's slight, lean figure would scarcely lead one to believe the wonderful powers of endurance and of rapid travelling over great distances, with very little food or water, which, like the majority of Somalis, he possessed. His dress consisted of a white cotton sheet, called in Somali a tobe, which is worn somewhat toga-fashion about the body; over his shoulder he carried, besides my pigsticking spear, a heavy broad-headed jobbing spear about six feet long. Somalis on the war-path would also carry a couple of lighter spears, which they can throw to a considerable distance with surprising accuracy. The heavy spear is only used at close quarters—a style of fighting to which, from all accounts, the Somalis are by no means partial, greatly preferring to fight at a distance, except when an opportunity of attacking an enemy by surprise—or, better still, treacherously—offers itself.

But to return to Abdullah, who, judging from all I heard and saw of him, was as plucky and trustworthy a fellow as one could wish for. A small, round shield for warding off spear thrusts (usually made of cow's hide), the face of which was neatly carved, and a long Somali knife, made of bad iron, in a sheath of white goatskin, worn round the middle, completed Abdullah's equipment. He was a cheery, intelligent fellow, and I would often get him to tell me about himself when leading a nomad life with his tribe before he saw civilization, such as it was, at Zaila. I remember on this occasion asking him if he had ever killed his man—a performance of some distinction in Somali ideas, entitling the slayer to wear an ostrich feather in his hair for some time after the event. Abdullah replied, with a triumphant grin, that he had, and, tucking up his tobe, showed me a large gash on his thigh, which, he said, he had received on one occasion when treacherously attacked from behind by a Somali of a hostile tribe.

"And what did you do?" I asked; and Abdullah, grinning all the while, proceeded to give me a pantomimic description of how he had driven his spear right through the man. "Margāyā, sahib, margāyā!" (he died), he added, in a most satisfied tone, which greatly amused me.

Chatting on in this way, we got over the ground, and forgot to think of how hot the sun overhead was. I dismounted now and then to take a shot at an occasional hare, and also managed to bag a bustard—a very different affair from shooting the Indian species. The African bird seemed to me a very unwary one, and it is easy enough to get within shot of it. Even when its fears are aroused, it rarely takes to flight immediately, but, as a rule, runs in the grass, and so is easily bagged by running in at it, and taking a shot as it slowly rises, flapping its big wings to get under way. I also got a few shots at some stray sand grouse. I had seen these birds in the morning, when the sun was hot, simply swarming round the wells, and if any one approached they would merely rise in a cloud and circle round the water, and again settle. It would have been mere useless slaughter to shoot them. The plain over which we were marching had a gradual ascent, terminating on the horizon in a long ridge of high ground, a short distance beyond which Abdullah said we should come to the wells of Uhdhawadiri, for the latter place was merely another wadi, where water was to be found by digging in the dried-up torrent bed.

As we approached the high ground, we passed by a karia, or Somali village. These villages are only temporary habitations, and are shifted from place to place, in order to obtain a sufficient amount of grass in the immediate neighbourhood for the grazing of their flocks of sheep and goats. A karia consists of a number of small huts constructed of reed mats, which are easily packed up on the backs of their camels, so that a move is very easily made. Except for a few women tending a large flock of sheep, and goats, the place had a very deserted appearance. Abdullah swaggered off to get khabar (news) of wart hog, and, no doubt, also to try his fascinations on these dusky Phyllises. He returned with the news that there were plenty of dofār all about Uhdhawadiri, and also to tell me that a large party of the Gadabursi (another Somali tribe, who are usually mounted) had made a raid but two days since on the large flock of camels belonging to this karia. A fight had taken place by the wells at Uhdhawadiri, in which several of the Eesa

Somalis had been killed, and the Gadabursi had ridden off, driving the Eesa camels before them. And now all the Eesa in the neighbourhood had gone off in pursuit to recapture their property, and likewise to revenge themselves. I felt rather disappointed at the news, for, had I only started a few days before, as I had originally intended, I should have witnessed a very good specimen of tribal feuds and raiding, such as are of frequent occurrence in Somali-land. We passed on, and were now about two miles from the ridge, when Abdullah suddenly stopped and caught hold of my pony's head, saying, "Dekho, sahib, dofār! bara dānt wallah," by which Abdullah meant to draw my attention to a boar with very large tushes close by. Almost as he spoke I saw the boar— such a beauty! with a glorious pair of tushes. He had evidently been feeding in some high grass not above four hundred yards away; but, having heard our voices, he was now, with raised head, staring boldly at us. Not caring to run the risk of losing the boar by riding him on the pony on which I was then mounted, in whose powers of speed and pluck to face a pig I was by no means confident, I told Abdullah to stay and watch our friend, and to follow him if he should move off, while I rode back in hot haste for my horse, whom my syce was leading some little distance in the rear, in company with the camel and the other men. Coming up to my syce, I took the saddle off the pony, and told him to put it on to the horse as quickly as possible. The latter seemed to guess instinctively the kind of fun before him, and became very frolicsome. As if seeing that his master was in a hurry, he appeared to take a mischievous delight in keeping him waiting, for he began prancing about, lashing out behind, and rearing up—in fact, behaving most disgracefully, thoroughly terrifying the syce, and keeping me on tenter-hooks with anxiety, for I could see the boar moving off at a run, so that I was fain to relieve my feelings in the choicest Anglo-Hindostani I could think of. At last I got the horse saddled, and, in another moment, was making him lay his legs to the ground in his very best style. The boar had got a long start, and was galloping, but, now that I was mounted, my mind was quite at ease; I felt sure he was mine. The nearest bit of jungle crowned the ridge I have mentioned, and that was quite two miles off; nor was the boar making in that direction, but was bounding gaily through the white, sun-withered grass of the plain, which stretched before us miles on miles, its white grasses in the distance taking a silvery light from the rays of the evening sun. Except for small bushes here and there, there was no other kind of cover in the line the boar was taking. "He hasn't a chance," thought I, as I settled my horse down into a steady gallop, for it was useless to send him along at top speed. The boar had a long start of us, and was now making the best of his way over the plain far ahead, but I knew I should come up with him, although the run would probably prove a long one. With the boar all to myself, and free from any fear of his escaping me in the jungle, I could afford to enjoy such moments to their full, and was far from wishing to shorten them. What glorious moments those were as I rattled over the ground at a spanking pace, feeling with delight every stride of my good nag, with his whole heart in the chase, going strongly and freely beneath me, while I watched the flying boar in front, and at length began to note with keen satisfaction how the distance between us shortened and shortened.

Two miles were covered ere the boar's speed began to flag perceptibly, but we now came up to him hand over hand. His gallop became a trot, as my nag overtook him with a rush. When just alongside, with my spear lowered for his shoulder, the boar turned and charged straight in at the horse; my spear struck him as he charged, and was buried high up on his back, close by the spine. From the concussion with which we met, the spear was forced out of my hand, and remained sticking upright in the boar's back as I passed on. Wheeling my nag round, I found the boar making for me. "What am I to do now?" thought I, and cursed myself for my clumsiness in losing the spear. "I must get it back—but how?" were my reflections, as I presented my horse's tail to the approaching boar, and rapidly retreated. On he came at a steady run, the spear standing almost upright in the middle of his back. It was a clear case of tables turned, and, while he continued to pursue me, there was nothing left for me but to judiciously run away. For some little distance the boar, looking very determined, followed me up, while I, looking back and wondering how I should recover the spear, continued to keep at a respectful distance from him. At length, seeing that he could not catch me, he gave up the pursuit, and turned off in another direction. I again became the pursuer, and rode after him, intending to try to pull the spear out of his back. But not a bit of it—the boar had no intention of letting me play that game. No sooner did I get near him than he would turn round and charge, with the confounded spear standing up from his back like a mainmast. It was impossible for me to get hold of the spear when he behaved in this manner; all that I could do was to promptly clear out of his way, hoping for a better chance at my next attempt. I might have recovered the spear if I had waited till he came alongside me, but I should have exposed my horse to the almost certainty of a bad rip, and this I did not want, especially at the outset, for it would have necessitated a return to Zaila, and so I deemed discretion the better part of valour in this case. Besides, I knew Abdullah would be following me up with the second spear at his very best speed. I noticed that the boar was steadily making for a clump of small bushes and high grass close by, and, however much he might be put out by my persistent and annoying efforts to recover my spear, he would doggedly resume the same course. We at length arrived at the high grass, and he sat down on his haunches, as if intending to rest himself. "Just the thing," thought I; "here we will wait for Abdullah. But what is he doing now?" I scarcely know which was greatest, my disgust or surprise, to see the boar retiring, stern foremost, into a hole hidden in the grass.

Facing me all the while, and looking at me as if to remark, "I have done you, I think," he slowly withdrew himself from before my eyes. This was too much for me, and I was off my horse like a shot, and seized the butt end of the spear, which was now pressed forward towards me, and endeavoured to run it deeper into his body, hoping somehow to stop his entire withdrawal. This I could not do, and the boar disappeared from view, all but his head and tushes, which were visible about half a foot from the edge of the hole. I hung on to the spear, the head of which still remained buried in the animal, and whether in doing so I prevented him vanishing altogether, or whether he was unable to do so from the depth of the hole, I do not know. However, thinking that the former might be the case, and that if I withdrew the spear he would escape me altogether, I had to content myself with merely keeping a tight hold on the spear, and praying for Abdullah's arrival.

I was very disappointed that the affair promised to have such a tame ending, and had faint hopes that the boar would get angry, and possibly charge out. Perhaps it was just as well for me that he did not, or could not, do so, as he would have caught me at a great disadvantage, being encumbered with my horse, whom I should have had to let go to defend myself, and heaven knows where the horse would have galloped to. I seemed to have stood there a long time, the sound of the boar's heavy breathing within the hole and of my horse champing his bit alone breaking the perfect stillness of the plain. At last Abdullah came up, all breathless from his long run, bringing with him my other spear. Giving him the horse's reins, and telling him to catch hold of the spear which was in the boar, I took the fresh spear, and began to prick the boar's nose and shoulders as an invitation to come out and fight, whereupon he seized the spear-head in his mouth, and left for me, as a reminiscence of the day, the marks of his teeth on the hard steel, and it was with the greatest difficulty I could free the spear. I renewed my efforts to draw him by prods more vicious than before, but without success, and I was very disgusted at the time with the boar for showing such a poor spirit in not coming out to fight, though I think now I may have done him an injustice, for he had certainly received a bad wound near the spine; and, besides, the hole was scarcely larger than his body, which, together with the spear which was buried in him, and held from outside by Abdullah, may have prevented him from rushing out to the attack. He had certainly proved himself game at the beginning of our acquaintance, and so I will give him the benefit of the doubt. However, I could not stay here all day, nor did I intend to lose such a pair of tushes, which I considered I had fairly earned; so I decided to give him his *coup de grâce* in the hole, and, with a few rapid thrusts into his body, brought the affair to an end. Tying the horse's reins round the animals tushes, Abdullah and I proceeded to drag the carcase from the hole, a by no means easy matter. However, we accomplished it at last, and the body of another wart hog lay before me.

I was indeed fortunate, for, although not of the same massive proportions as my adversary of the evening before, he seemed to be a full-grown animal, and had the finest pair of tushes I was destined to get. The upper pair measured over 9½ inches along the outer curve, and were almost as thick as those of the first boar; the lower pair were of the same length, and as sharp as a knife. I regret I took no measurements of the beast's size, but I should think this boar stood 30 inches, and no more. My men having come up, the head was cut off, and, after being held before my horse's nose, who gave a snort of satisfaction, was packed on the camel. When the Somali pony was brought near the carcase of the boar he trembled with fright, and nearly tore himself free in his terror. I was very glad that I had not tried conclusions with my late friend when mounted on him.

## CHAPTER III.

WE resumed our way towards Uhdhawadiri. On reaching the ridge of high ground, before us lay, to the left, a beautiful park-like country studded with clumps of bushes and small trees; and not far from where we stood the light-coloured, graceful forms of a herd of African gazelle, grazing, were visible amidst the dark green of the jungle. Here and there the bushes grew very close together, forming large patches of covert, which, looked at from a pigsticker's point of view, were not desirable. To our right rolled the great plain, covered with its whitish grass, stretching away to the horizon, and looking in the far-off distance, under the glow of the setting sun, like some silvery sea; and as I stood there and watched the great red sun as it sank down beyond it, I thought I had never beheld a scene so full of wild and desolate grandeur, so overpowering in its vastness and drear solitude, as this great expanse of sun-parched, waterless plain that rolled on before me its billows of silvery grass. Turning somewhat to the left, we made towards the more wooded country through which the wadi of Uhdha-wadiri ran.

I was just thinking of how I should enjoy dinner and a good rest, when Abdullah, who had gone a little distance ahead, came running back to me with the khabar that he had just seen a drove of twelve dofār grazing not far ahead. Thoughts of dinner and rest were thus put to flight, and I rode back quickly to the syce to again change the saddle on to the horse. It was soon done, and I cantered in the direction that Abdullah pointed out; but ride where I might, alas! no drove of pigs could I find; they had, no doubt, got into some of the patches of jungle I have mentioned. Though, of course, disappointed, I thought it was perhaps just as well, for it was getting dusk, and I should most probably have lost myself in riding after the pig—a by no means desirable occurrence in such a howling wilderness, where, unacquainted with the country, one might wander for days in search of water until one dropped, so rare are these precious watering-places in the dry season.

I returned to where my people were halted, and we continued our way, and soon struck the wadi, which we followed along its sandy bed until we came to the wells. My tent was soon pitched, the camel unloaded, and, after a not particularly luxurious meal, at which my dog kept me company (by-the-by, I had forgotten to mention her presence), I turned in, well content with my first two days' experience of pig-sticking in Africa. And here I may as well bring my account of this pigsticking expedition to a close, as my luck seemed to have changed, for during the five days I stayed at Uhdha-wadiri, I only came across a couple of sows with a drove of squeakers. I bagged the largest sow, after a pleasant run, without any more noteworthy incident than that, the run having taken me back close by my camp, just as I had severely wounded the sow, who was moving off slowly, my little fox terrier, catching sight of me, came tearing towards me, and joined in the pursuit, keeping alongside the sow, and barking furiously at her hind quarters. Besides being in my way, I was rather alarmed for her safety, but unnecessarily so, for the poor pig was far too much concerned with my intentions to be able to take any notice of such an insignificant little person. The sow sported tushes measuring, both in the upper and lower jaw, five inches—a point on which the African sow differs remarkably from the Indian, which rarely shows any at all.

On my return to Zaila, I found that the parental care of the political authorities disapproved of my entering so far into the country with so small an escort, so I was compelled to confine my pursuit of the wart hog to places not more than ten to fourteen miles distant, which, however, did not prevent me from having very good sport, as the number of wart hog that I speared, as given previously, shows. *Apropos* of the incident I have related of the boar running to earth, I was soon afterwards to have another very practical proof that these animals do live in holes. When in Aden I had heard the subject mentioned by those who had shot in the Somali country, but they were more or less incredulous about it, and seemed to put it down to a bit of romancing on the part of the Somalis. The rather amusing incident that happened to me, which I am going to relate, sufficiently convinced me, if I required convincing after my former experience, that the wart hog do inhabit holes.

It was in this way. One morning I had ridden out to Warabōd on pigsticking bent, but had been entirely unsuccessful in my search. While riding through the jungle, in company with Abdullah and two other Somalis, on my way back to Zaila, very hot, and far from sweet-tempered from having had no luck, we came across a large hole in a small mound crowned with bushes. Abdullah went up to it, and began examining the ground, and then called out to me that there were very fresh marks of pig about the mouth of the hole. It was very hot, and I was not at all keen to get off my horse; moreover, I had often come across similar holes with the pugs of pig near them, and had lighted fires to smoke them out, and devised other methods, such as throwing lighted squibs and firing off blank cartridges into the holes, in the hopes of driving out a possible inhabitant, but always with no result, and I was becoming rather sceptical on the subject of the wart hog living underground after all. However, Abdullah was all keenness on my trying my luck again; so I dismounted, and gave the horse to one of the Somalis, and while Abdullah danced and stamped on the top of the mound, and uttered unearthly yells, I stood at the mouth, and lazily thrust my spear down it. It was evidently a deep hole, for my spear almost disappeared, without apparently striking anything. "Kuch na hai, Abdullah" (there is nothing here), said I, withdrawing the spear and carelessly ramming it down again. The words were hardly out of my mouth when a hoarse "Woof, woof," resounded from the depths of the hole, like the bellowing of some beast from the infernal regions, and as I, staggering backwards and clutching my spear to shorten it for the encounter, stumbled and fell clean over on my back, two big, black bodies seemed to literally fly out of the hole, and leaped over my prostrate body, I still grabbing at the spear to defend myself. If ever a man was completely astonished in his life, I was at that moment.

Abdullah uttered a howl of dismay, and rushed up to me to know if I was hurt. Hurt

I was not, but very indignant, and in a second I was on my horse and tearing like mad after those pigs. They were a boar and a sow. I singled out the boar, and, after a very sharp run, wiped out the indignity that I had suffered while sprawling at the mercy of himself and mate. He was a youngish boar, with tushes not more than six inches long, but a rare fellow for jinking. How those two animals managed to live in one hole, without one being suffocated, has always remained a mystery to me. I can only imagine that the hole inside must have assumed larger proportions, or branched off into different holes, though this supposition is quite contrary to my experience of these abodes of the wart hog; for afterwards I had several dug into, and I never saw any that were wide enough for two abreast, or that branched off into two different compartments.

On one occasion, while riding about the plain by Warabōd, I came across a very fine boar, who dashed off immediately on catching sight of me. It was indeed quite remarkable how soon my evil-disposed intentions became known to the wart hog inhabiting Warabōd. They never now stopped to look at me twice, as my first acquaintances among them used to do. I put spurs to my horse, and pursued him hotly; it was one of the fastest runs I ever had. Just before he reached a little clump of bushes growing on a hillock, I came alongside, and speared him as he jinked, the point, it seemed to me, entering his stomach rather far back. As I brought the horse round to renew the attack, I found the boar in the act of retiring stern foremost down a hole in the bushes, and, as I rode sharply forward to the hole, he disappeared from view. Highly disgusted at such an unsportsmanlike proceeding on the part of the boar, I took up a position behind the hillock, and watched it quietly, hoping that the boar might emerge from his refuge when he thought the coast was clear. The sun went down, and a glorious moon rose in the heavens, lighting up the whole plain with its beautiful light, and still I waited on; for the moon was so brilliant, every bush and tree standing out so clearly on the moonlit plain, that it seemed to me quite possible to ride if he would only turn up, and to spear a boar by the light of the moon was a novelty in pigsticking I was anxious to try. I had attempted it once before, although unsuccessfully, when encamped out for the night by the wells of Warabōd. While sitting in my tent after dinner, one of my men came to tell me that they heard the pig at the water; so I had the horse quickly saddled, and rode towards the spot. The sound of my horse's hoofs had, however, given the alarm, for all I saw was the dark form of a wart hog flying through the bushes. I gave chase, but, as the moon was not full, and the pig had got a good start of me, I soon lost sight of him. But on another occasion, at a later period than that about which I am writing, when stationed at Berbera (also on the Somali coast) I had a capital ride by moonlight after a large hyæna. I was awakened one night, while sleeping outside the house, by a sentry close by, who brought me khabar of a couple of hyænas on the prowl not far off—a fact I could easily learn for myself when once awake, from the infernal baying of all the pariah dogs of the town—I had my horse saddled immediately, and, having tucked my pyjamas into a pair of long boots, and caught up a spear from the wall, I was soon careering after one of the hyænas, who legged it for the open plain lying outside the town. I remember it was a lovely night. So magnificent was the moonlight that I was able to ride the hyæna at a fair gallop for quite two miles, the ground being fairly covered with small bushes and very stony. Once I was almost on the point of spearing him, but he jinked, and made back for the sea. I followed, but lost ground in having to descend a rather awkward place. When I came up with him again I found him sitting in the wash of the tide, evidently thoroughly blown; but as I rode up to spear him, he got up and ran along the wet sand, where I could only follow with difficulty, and I eventually lost sight of him amongst the rocks.

But, to return to my story. I waited by the hole for quite two hours, and then my patience became exhausted, and I gave it up; but thinking that there was just the possibility of the wound the boar had received proving a mortal one, I told Abdullah to heap some branches over the mouth of the hole, and decided to come on the morrow to see if he was still there. The next day I was not able to go out pigsticking, but on the following one started at noon, taking with me four Somalis, armed with spades, on the off-chance of finding the boar still in the hole. We reached the place early in the afternoon, and, to my great delight, there were the branches over the hole just as we had placed them. Nothing could be seen of the boar, but in there he was sure enough, and my Somalis set to work to dig him out, while I rode off in search of others. Coming back about sunset, I found them still at work; they had opened up the hole, which was an exceedingly long one, with many turns and windings, for some distance, and said they thought they could see the boar's tushes. So I got down, and crept along the course of the hole they had dug up, and in the darkness I saw a glimmer of something white, which I rapped with my spear; the sound it gave back left me no doubt of its being the boar's tushes. Encouraging my men to fresh exertions by promises of extra baksheesh, they started to open up the hole further. After some time, when the earth was cleared away, we came on the boar's head; the poor beast was evidently in a dying state, and must have been without food or water since I had speared him; so, taking my rifle, I put a bullet in his head as the quickest way of ending his sufferings.

The tushes of the African sow run at times to a considerable length; and I was very often deceived at first sight as to the sex of the animals on this account. However, I always considered the sow perfectly fair sport, since she was as well armed as many an Indian boar; and I never hesitated to ride one if there was not a boar on the ground.

One of the most determined of pigs that I ever had the pleasure of meeting was an old sow, sporting a pair of such curly tushes as would have caused envy in the heart of many a boar. I met her in company with another sow and a drove of squeakers one evening while riding about the Warabōd plain, as usual accompanied by the faithful Abdullah. The whole drove, catching sight of me, dashed off towards the jungle. It was a pretty sight to see the little pigs running with all their might alongside the big forms of the two sows, who proportioned their pace to the running powers of the little ones. Away went the squeakers, with all their little tails held merrily in the air, in ridiculous imitation of their elders, uttering a chorus of squeaks and squeals—sounds that were indeed as pleasant music in my ears as I rode after them. The larger sow was evidently the mother of the squeakers, and her tushes were very ordinary ones; so I singled out the other sow, probably the grandmother, a tough, wiry, bad-tempered-looking old girl, with the beautiful, curly pair of tushes that I have mentioned, and looking as if she would show plenty of fight if annoyed. I was not mistaken. After a smart run I ran alongside to spear; but she jinked, and I missed her. Pulling up my horse, after failing to spear, and looking round, I found, to my surprise, the sow no longer in flight, but standing still and looking at me. And now, while the rest of the drove sought safety in the jungle, this brave old sow stood her ground and prepared to give me battle. Delighted with her pluck, I wished to give her every chance; so as she, tossing her head and making her long mane fly about, came charging up at my horse's chest, I decided to meet her charge at a standstill, levelling my spear in order to clear her head and strike her in the back. Five successive times did she gallantly charge straight at my horse, only to be stopped, literally at his knees, by the spear point entering her back close to the hind quarters. Once I forced her right back on her haunches, and on withdrawing my spear she retired only to again return to the attack. For the sixth time she came on as bravely as ever, though staggering from her wounds. This time my spear, badly directed, struck her on the head, instead of in the back, and so failed to stop her. With a vicious squeal she ran in between the legs of my horse, who had stood her charges all this while as steady as if on parade, trusting entirely to me to stop her. But now that I had failed to do so, he took his defence into his own hands, or rather legs.

There now ensued a short and sharp scuffle. The snorting and plunging of my horse mingled with the vicious squeals of the sow, while the dull thud, thud of my nag's heels told me that the sow was not having it all her own way. She was evidently catching it rather hot. All that I could do was to sit tight and endeavour, by a plentiful use of the spurs, to get my horse clear of the sow.

Abdullah, who had been standing a little distance off watching the fight, now greatly alarmed for his sahib's safety, came running up, crying out "Khabardār!" with every intention of going for the pig with his spear, and very reluctantly obeyed the order to keep away that I shouted at him. At length I managed to get the horse clear of the sow, whom I left standing shaking her head, and looking as if she had not altogether relished her warm reception.

Not knowing what wounds my horse might have received in the scrimmage, I charged down on the sow, intending to bring the fight to an end as sharp as possible. My spear entered the hind part of her body, and rolled her over; but, game to the last, the brave beast struggled up on to her haunches to continue the fight. Wheeling round, I again rode down on her, spearing her clean through the body, and, unfortunately, breaking the spear shaft in doing so.

With a wild scream she rolled over dead. I jumped off to examine my horse, and was very pleased to find that he had received nothing worse than a slight cut on the hind leg above the hock. A feather, indeed, in that sow's cap, if she could have known it; for she was the only pig that succeeded in cutting my horse. The upper tushes of this sow measured nine inches, the under pair six inches. The tushes of the upper jaw are not of the same remarkable thickness as those of the boar; they are about as thick as the upper tushes of the Indian boar.

## CHAPTER IV.

The lonely existence led at Zaila was occasionally enlivened by the short visits of a gunboat from Aden, and I was only too glad to get some of the officers to come out shooting or pigsticking with me, though, as a general rule, I certainly prefer to pigstick by myself rather than in company. Riding for first spear, of course, has a great charm, but after all it is not always the most deserving who wins the tushes, luck, or a good horse, as often as not winning against hard-riding. The greater charm which I find in pigsticking alone is the plucky fight that the boar will often show at the end of the run, and the certainty of having the boar all to one's self, if he does show fight, gives a wonderfully keen zest to the ride.

It seems to me that the fight with the pig is utterly spoilt if it has to be shared with others; for the odds against the boar at bay, fighting for his life, are too great where there are two or more spears on the field to contend with.

But, *chacun à son goût*. I know many will not agree with me. Zaila, however, is not a place where one could afford to despise company when it was obtainable. So one day I started, in company with three officers of H.M.S. *Woodlark*, for Warabōd, where we intended to spend Christmas week shooting and pigsticking, taking it in turns to do the latter; for the only decent mounts that we could raise in the town were my horse and a nice-looking Harrar pony, lent to me by a Greek merchant of the place, which promised to be equal to facing a pig. While riding over the plain by Warabōd I noticed a small cloud of dust moving along amongst the bushes at some little distance from us. Thinking that some animal must be the cause of the dust, as there was scarcely a breath of wind, I cantered quickly towards the spot, and was rewarded for my trouble. A nice-looking sow broke covert, going away at a rattling pace. I stopped to give a wave of my spear and a "halloo" to one of the party, who was on the other mount, and gave chase. Never in all my life did I meet such a troublesome little friend as that sow. She gave me an exceedingly long and fast run, and then how she did jink! A dozen times at least did I ride into her, only to miss her; jinking, dodging, and twisting among the bushes till I thought the devil was in her. My horse was getting quite blown, and I was not much better. Again making a spurt, I came alongside of her. Again she jinked, but this time right across my horse. My patience was all gone; and, though knowing what a risky and foolish thing I was doing, I could not resist the temptation. I leant forward and speared her, as she crossed me, fairly in the body. Crack went the shaft of my spear, as my horse, at full gallop, struck it with his chest, and I only just saved bringing him down on his head by letting go my hold of the spear. The spear was clean broken, but I had the consolation of seeing that I had brought that troublesome sow to book at last. I had rolled her completely over, and she now lay squealing on the ground, with the broken spear buried in her side. Anxious to recover the spear and polish her off, I jumped off my horse and went towards the sow, whom I thought to be *in extremis*. But I was in far too great a hurry, for up she got and came for me at a run. The spear was sticking out from behind, so that I could not possibly get hold of that, and I was without even a hunting knife to defend myself. So, to turn tail and retreat, as rapidly as my horse would allow me, was all that there was left for me to do. My horse would only move at the very slowest trot, and every moment I thought the pig would catch me. I did not want to let go of him, for I knew that he would run away, nor was there time to mount, for the pursuing sow was almost at the horse's heels. Fortunately for me, she could only follow up very slowly; the spear, buried in her side, and dragging on the ground, no doubt must have impeded her movements. Ever looking round to see if the sow was gaining on me, and with a most uncomfortable fear that her sharp little tushes would make themselves felt in some part of my person, I thus continued my flight, with very little breath left in me, and fast losing that from the violent tugs I gave at the horse's bridle to get him to move faster. For my horse would only follow at a most reluctant trot, evidently not understanding such an extraordinary proceeding as himself and master running away from a pig.

I was just meditating on a dodge round the horse, in hopes that the sow might pass on, when my friend turned up, and so put an end to this comical scene—for so it must have proved to anybody but the person most concerned. The sow, seeing a new arrival, made off towards some thick jungle close by. My friend gave chase, but failed to spear her, and she got off, not only with her tushes, which I considered fairly my own, but with my spear as well. A week afterwards a Somali brought the spear, covered with dried blood, into Zaila. He told me that he had found it at the mouth of a hole, and I have no doubt the sow died of the wound she had received, for it was a severe one.

On another occasion, B., of H.M.S. *Woodlark*,

and I were riding about the Warabōd plain in search of pig. We were keeping about a quarter of a mile apart, in order to cover as much ground as possible, and still keep each other in view. Having ridden in this manner for some distance, keenly scanning the country in all directions, I had begun to think that there was to be no sport for us that day, when, on looking in B.'s direction, I saw that he was galloping, and, though I could see nothing, I was able to guess that he had come across pig. I rode very hard in the direction I saw that B. was taking, and at length, between the clumps of bushes, I caught flying glimpses of a couple of pig sailing over the ground in fine style, with B. going hard and close up with them. Fortunately, the pig rather inclined to my direction, and soon B. and I were galloping alongside each other with a couple of fine boars keeping together a little distance ahead.

Being the better mounted, I was able to spurt ahead, and singled out the boar whose tushes seemed the largest for my own special attention. Finding themselves pressed, the boars separated, the one which I had selected almost doubling back in the direction he had come. I followed him closely, leaving B. to render an account of his companion. Although fairly close on him, I was not able to spurt in and spear, for he was still galloping fast, and seemed full of running, while my horse, I could feel, was rather blown from the pace at which I had sent him along from the start. The troublesome twisting and dodging course that the boar took between the bushes was far more trying than a straight run would have been.

At length, spurring my horse hard, I rode in at the boar, and tried to spear. He, however, jinked as I came alongside, and I merely succeeded in pricking him. This would never do, for my horse seemed far more blown than the pig; so, as we were still some distance from the jungle, I pulled up to breathe him before continuing the run.

As I did so, I saw the boar had stopped also, his anger, I suppose, aroused at the scratch I had given him. He now came trotting towards me, as if intending a charge. I, with lowered spear, stood to receive him, but, evidently thinking better of it, he suddenly turned off and trotted slowly away. I think he must have thought he had frightened us, for he was not hurrying himself in the least. After giving my nag a minute or more of breathing time, I rode sharply to the boar's right, determined to settle him off hand. Then, wheeling my horse round, I rode him at full gallop at the boar's flank, just as he emerged into an open space between some clumps of bushes. Too late he tried to avoid me, as I rode straight down on him, sending my spear sheer through his body, and as my horse cleared the boar I saw the bright steel of the spearhead standing out clear behind his left shoulder. The boar was rolled over. He staggered up again; a shudder seemed to pass through his body, and with a gasp he fell over dead.

Curious to know how B. had succeeded, I tied my handkerchief to the highest bush I could find, in order to mark the spot, and rode off in the direction he had taken. I soon came across him not very far from where I had killed. He was dismounted, and looking regretfully into a hole at the foot of a hillock overgrown with bushes, and so I easily guessed his misfortune.

He had speared his boar once, but, less fortunate than I, his animal had come across the hole and disappeared down it.

There were several holes in the mound besides the one into which the boar had gone, and we thought it very probable that they would be connected with each other; and so, in hopes of being able to drive the boar out, I rode back to our followers for a shot gun, leaving B. on guard over the boar's retreat. Returning, I proceeded to fire down the various holes, while B. stood ready mounted to ride if the boar should make a bolt out. At length I heard something come out and hide in the bushes. Thinking this must be the boar, I called out to B. to be ready, and, taking my spear began to peer cautiously into the thick bushes. But at first I could see nothing, and yet I was sure an animal of some sort was hidden in them. At length, hearing something moving in the thickest part of the bushes, I thrust my spear into them, and out rushed, close by me, only a big porcupine. Spear in hand, I gave chase, thinking I might as well possess myself of his quills. But I found that in riding boots I was no match for the porcupine, who was legging it like a hare, evidently furiously angry, from the horrid noise he was making with his bristles. He looked so comical as he ran that I lost the little remaining breath I had in laughing, and so had to call on B. to ride after him and spear him, if he could. B. endeavoured to do so, but the pony, who had faced a pig well enough, shied so at the noise of the quills that B. could not get him near the porcupine, who thus escaped us both by scuttling into another hole.

Night was fast coming on when we gave up all hope of driving B.'s boar out of the hole. Our followers with the camel having turned up, we returned to the spot where my dead boar lay. I found that the jackals had been there already, and saw several of the culprits skulking among the surrounding bushes. An amateur photographer having promised to take a photograph of a wart hog if I brought one into Zaila, B. and I (we could get no help from the Somalis) after some trouble, hoisted the carcase on to the camel's back and tied it there. Then, leaving our men to come on with the camel, we started to ride back, trusting to find our way under the beautiful starlight, and soon struck the track leading to Zaila, now grown so familiar to me in many a ride by the wondrous moonlight and starlight of those glorious nights in Africa. I took the following measurements of the boar, who was a medium-sized animal—

|  | Ft. | In. |
|---|---|---|
| Length from tip of snout to root of tail | 4 | $2\frac{3}{4}$ |
| Length of tail | 2 | 0 |
| Height | 2 | 6 |
| Length of head | 1 | 5 |
| Span of tushes of upper jaw | 0 | 10 |
| Tushes of upper jaw | 0 | $8\frac{1}{4}$ |
| Tushes of lower jaw | 0 | $7\frac{3}{4}$ |
| Measurement round thickest part of upper tush | 0 | 4 |
| Measurement round thickest part of lower tush | 0 | $2\frac{1}{2}$ |
| Weight of upper pair of tushes | $9\frac{1}{2}$ oz. |  |
| Weight of lower pair of tushes | 3 ,, |  |

The weight of each upper tush—viz. $4\frac{3}{4}$ oz.—will give some idea of its massiveness. From the tip to about two-thirds of its length it is solid ivory. The tushes of the lower jaw, like those of the Indian boar, are hollow throughout.

A Somali, who had come in from the interior, once brought me some wart hogs' tushes, which I bought of him. These actually measured 13 inches, and have a proportional increase in girth and weight. The Somali told me that he had picked them up in the jungle in the hilly country near Gildessa, a place on the kāfila route to Harrar; so evidently the African wart hog of the hills has still more remarkable tushes than those of the plains, and, from what I could gather from Somalis, is a larger animal. I am sorry to say that the amateur in photography proved to be an amateur indeed in that art, for, when the negatives were sent to Aden to be developed, it was, I heard, quite impossible to distinguish the boar's head from his tail. I regretted this very much, for I think a likeness of the African wart hog would have been acceptable to those interested in natural history. The structure of this animal's teeth is, I think, remarkable. The whole range of back teeth on each side of the upper and lower jaws are a connected row of cylindrically-shaped cells filled in with an osseous substance.

There is one point I have forgotten to mention about the wart hog, viz. its powerlessness to turn its head to either side to the same extent that other animals can. This is, of course, owing to the almost entire absence of neck in this animal. Often, when chasing a wart hog, I had noticed that he would carry at times his snout uplifted in the air, and turned slightly to one side, as he ran—a proceeding which gave him an extremely comical appearance. I never quite understood why the animal should do this, until on one occasion when I had speared a sow, who managed, however, to escape me down a hole. On the chance of her coming out again, I had taken up a position behind some bushes in rear of the hole, which I carefully watched. My patience was this time rewarded, for after some time a snout and a pair of tushes began to protrude themselves from the hole, a head soon followed, and then a body, and at length I saw with much satisfaction the whole animal, sitting on her haunches, at the mouth of the hole. First she reconnoitred well to her front, and as much on each side of her as she could manage; then up went her snout in the air, in the quaintest manner imaginable, turning her nose round to either side. Then it dawned on me what she was up to—she was evidently taking a squint behind her. I was well concealed amongst the bushes, and fortunately my horse was keeping perfectly still. Satisfied in her mind that the coast was clear of the enemy, she got up and trotted off, doubtless homewards. Poor deluded sow, had you but made a more careful examination of those bushes you had been enjoying existence still, for, when well away from your place of refuge, down came the enemy on you and bagged you.

I was never able to decide whether the wart hog made their own holes, or whether they appropriated to themselves the abodes of other animals. I came across an account by Gordon Cumming of how he once chased a wart hog which, just as he was on the point of shooting, he says, disappeared down a large disused ant-bear hole. The Somalis used to tell me that the holes were the work of the hyæna and jackal, but I am inclined to think that they are the wart hog's own manufacture. The habit of making large excavations in the ground would account for the size and strength of the tushes in the upper jaw, with which they are armed. Further, the remarkable strength and stoutness of the wart hog's upper tushes, in contrast with those of the Indian boar, who makes his lair under some covert of bushes, seem to point to the work for which the African boar requires them. These holes were certainly great drawbacks to the pig-sticking I got in the Somali country, which in other points was quite perfect; they frequently spoilt the ride, but, on the other hand, hard riding was absolutely necessary from start to finish, for there was no knowing when one of these most undesirable holes might turn up. My runs, therefore, as a rule, were very fast and short. After my Indian spears were broken, I took to using the Somali jobbing spear in the Bengal style. Its broad head, I found, gave a frightful wound, a pig rarely getting much further after it had been once driven well home. It was, however, an awkward weapon to meet a charging pig with, being very badly balanced for that purpose.

Abdullah was highly pleased with my performances with his native weapon, and on my leaving Zaila he came to me and asked me to take as a present his own spear. Nothing would induce him to take money to buy another one; but on my offering him my old hunting-knife, his face lighted up with delight, and so a satisfactory exchange was made. Abdullah came down with me to the ship, and, as I said good-bye to him, the good fellow, with almost tears in his eyes, said to me in his broken Hindostani, "Pichche ao sahib; pichche ao dofār mārne ke wasti" (Come back, sahib; come back to kill more dofār).

THE END.